MUSIC WITH WORDS

Virgil Thomson

MUSIC WITH WORDS

A Composer's View

Yale University Press New Haven & London

Designed by Richard Hendel
and set in Galliard type
by G&S Typesetters, Austin, Texas.
Printed in the United States of America

Library of Congress Cataloging-in-Publication Data
Thomson, Virgil, 1896–
Music with words : a composer's view / Virgil Thomson.
   p.   cm.
Bibliography: p.
Includes index.
ISBN 0-300-04505-0
1. Vocal music—20th century—History and criticism.
2. Composition.   3. Libretto.   4. Opera.   I. Title.
      ML1406.T5   1989
   784'.028—dc19   89-30709
                  CIP
                  MN

10 9 8 7 6 5 4 3 2 1

CONTENTS

MUSICAL EXAMPLES

PREFACE

This is not a textbook. It is merely a group of essays about vocal music, as composers face the writing of it, especially to English words.

Most of these pieces are new; the two longest are older. Chapter 1 is a lecture that I have been giving in clubs and colleges for over fifty years. I have not previously allowed its publication lest distribution in that form injure its earning-power; but I have rewritten it to refresh its language about every ten or twelve years. The next to last piece, a discourse about opera, was published in *Parnassus,* a quarterly devoted to the criticism of poetry.

The chapters do not need to be read consecutively, nor do they make up a syllabus. When I have held classes in vocal composition I have used their materials, but my main procedure there was simply to read over the music that the students had composed and then help them, if I could, to improve it. This method resembles what law schools call "the case system." As a result, the book presents itself less as a program of skills to be progressively acquired than as a body of knowledge which can be browsed in, remembered perhaps, used when needed, and little by little encompassed.

Whether the suggestions here offered are practical can best be learned by trying them out. Whether my opinions about music are in the long run convincing may take some time to learn. I admit right off, however, that my personal views of vocal music are not those commonly held regarding the English-language repertory.

I give far more attention to opera, for example, than would seem to be justified by the meager success that that form has enjoyed in our tongue. And I have not treated extensively our choral music, which has been since the fourteenth century (in Latin) and since the mid-sixteenth century (in English) one of the glories of Europe. Even in America, with our gifted colonials and our inventive folkways—our fuguing-tunes and white spirituals, our blues, show-songs and commercial pops, not to speak of experimental modernisms by Charles Ives and many others—singing in all its forms has been a favored indulgence.

These outpourings, especially in the pops and in the folk field, have been so thoroughly written about already as to need no comment from me. Even the concert song, in spite of its constant practice by our best composers, does not seem to have followed in recent times any major creative direction. Nor has it in England either, for that matter.

More and more I tend to find opera, which is the grandest, the most varied, and the richest of all theatrical forms, to be also the most encompassing among vocal possibilities. Getting it into English and making it stick there, to make the writing of English operas seem a worthy way of life, that I think is the preoccupation today of forward-looking composers in both England and America.

Symphonic composition, either there or here, I have little faith in. And chamber music everywhere is chiefly tolerable today as an experiment in methodology. Writing more solo works for the pianoforte, the organ, the violin, or the cello is looking backward to the masters who by creating for these instruments with so comprehensive a palette actually patented, and exhausted, the gamut of feelings that anybody now living can find urgent in the sound of those instruments. There is still fun to be had with woodwinds maybe, just maybe. And the concert song in English is, I fear, a never-never land from which few invaders bring home booty.

But opera composed in English is still unfinished business, worth working at, and possibly, in view of what has happened since 1930 both in the United Kingdom and with us, possibly alive and certainly wiggling. These thoughts may explain the lack of a reasoned balance in my consideration of the field.

They do not justify, of course, the quoting of examples uniquely from my own works. That is a liberty I have taken because they are the repertory I know best. And they actually illustrate most of the situations mentioned in the text. Any student or any instructor can, I am sure, think of others no less apt.

CHAPTER ONE

A Formal Introduction to the Subject

The union of poetry and music is older than recorded time. In ancient Greece they were inseparable. All music had words, and all the plays were sung. Nowadays poetry and music live apart. I am speaking of classical music and of poetry for reading, not folk tunes nor the ditties we call "popular." Nearly the whole of our rhymed folklore, as well as the commercial product, still consists of words *and* music.

In popular music, both folk and commercial, a tune may well be older than its verses. Also, many a tunesmith and his lyricist work together. But more commonly, in Tin Pan Alley just as in the backwoods, almost any song begins its life as a melody.

In the world of serious music, on the other hand, it is poems that get music fitted to them. Sometimes, I know, new words are run up for old melodies, and beloved airs from oratorio and opera have been known to be used again, sometimes by their own composers, George Frideric Handel for instance. But nobody, literally nobody ever tries to create an oratorio or opera by first composing an instrumental score, in the hope that someone someday will put a libretto under it.

In performance, things are again reversed. The words of a pop song, though the last element to be added, have first rights toward being understood. Vocalism, in this practice, is less important than enunciation. With art music, on the other hand, beauty of tone may well be the objective. One has to have words to write a concert song, but in performance these are not always easy to distinguish.

All the same, it is pleasanter to understand what music is saying than merely to enjoy the sound that it makes. So if songs really need words (as indeed they mostly do, since the human voice without them is just another wind instrument) then there has to be in the marriage of words and music a basic compatibility in which the text's exact shape and purpose dominate the union, or seem to. I say seem to, because actually a large part of music's

1

contribution lies in the emotional timings, the urgencies about continuity, the whole pacing and moving-forwardness of the composition that only music can provide.

When a composer lays out a text for musical setting, he does something like what an actor would do preparing to read it aloud. He spaces it for its natural word-groups, phrases, sentences, paragraphs, periods. Clarity of meaning is his first objective; second, a reasonable amount of feeling may be laid on. But not overindulgently, we hope, since enunciation must always take precedence. Indeed, we suspect any speaker of insincerity who assumes an undue expressivity, like a radio announcer trying to sell us something.

Actually the composer who simply scans his text may be doing it better service than the one who competes with it to assure us how deeply he feels about it. The basis of communication, in other words, is a plain verbal prosody. Enrichment of this through apt vocal turn, instrumental illustration, even a grandly symphonic structure, all the devices that give music its larger life, are welcome, but only so far as they do not obscure the meaning or misplace an emphasis.

Tennyson boasted that he knew the prosody of every word in English except *scissors*. Myself I do not feel so confident. The word *banana,* for instance, may be easy for a poet. But it can be troublesome for music, as in the once-popular refrain

<blockquote>Yes, we have no bananas.</blockquote>

Later we shall analyze the vowels in this word.

In analyzing any text we must remember that language is not just one word after another. It is printed that way, but not so spoken or sung. In performance it is an arbitrarily ordered string of vocal noises. These may vary in length and loudness; but each is only one kind of sound, represented by a symbol of its own in the International Phonetic Alphabet. And not one of these sounds, heard alone, means anything. When ordered into recognizable rows they are called words, and a list of these, printed out, makes a dictionary. Also, words are attached by common consent to meanings, often to several meanings. But the meaning of a discourse is not the result of their looking in print like a string of words. It is the result of their being organized into word-groups.

These groups sound like words, and they operate like words in the sense that they have accents and durations that cannot, at least in English, be altered or interrupted without changing the meaning. Nor can they be punctuated, though compound words may accept a hyphen.

"How do you do?," for instance, is a word-group admitting no change in the order or accentuation of its sounds. It means consequently not at all what it looks like, a string of words, but what it sounds like, a pattern of phonemes. In this agreed upon pattern lies its meaning. A listing of the phonemes familiar to Europe and the Americas is called the International Phonetic Alphabet. But of that too, more later.

To show how a literary text falls into meaningful word-groups, let me cite the opening lines of Milton's sonnet "On His Blindness":

> When I consider how my light is spent
> E're half my days in this dark world and wide,

What are the word-groups here? "When I consider" is the first; this represents a thought minimally stated. "How my light is spent" is another; it is almost divisible into two thoughts, but not quite. "E're half my days" is clearly the next statement, followed by "in this dark world," and finally "and wide," this last an extention of "dark world," but independent of it.

Nowhere in these lines is any single word meaningful. Only word-groups have that kind of reality. And to maintain its reality each of these must be pronounced without interruption. Moreover, the sonnet itself, read aloud, is not a sequence of its lines or of its words, only of its word-groups. Any string of these can be assembled into a phrase or cut up, if the meaning permits, into short sentences or into exclamations. But they can no more be split up into words than words themselves can be thought of as just letters.

Before being set to music, a text, any text, needs to be mapped into meaningful word-groups, very much as has been done above with the first two lines of Milton's sonnet. After that, they need to be examined in detail, for speaking or for singing, as simply vowels and consonants.

I must explain at this point my aim, which is to establish a method of operation for vocal writing in English or in American. These languages can be considered for singing, I think, as identical. They differ in speech, of course. Winston Churchill and Franklin Roosevelt, for example, did not speak at all alike, though in both cases their diction was clearly upper-class. On the other hand, I defy anyone to find a noticeable difference between Leontyne Price's way of singing English and Kathleen Ferrier's, since both used a singer's approach to the idiom. And it is artists of this class, plus the studios that train them, that exemplify the performance conventions now current.

These conventions, I may add, have not changed much in the last four centuries. A need for constantly explaining them to composers does arise, however, because musicians, with their many differences of education and of racial background, as well as with the heavy preponderance of instrumental music that dominates our modern culture, are often out of touch with vocal traditon.

I may also suggest that the study of linguistics, nowadays a branch of philosophy, is not likely to be of much service to musicians. Phonetics, yes. That is of value for examining word-groups and their regional variations, also for using the International Phonetic Alphabet, should such need arise. A grave trouble with phoneticians is that their inveterate preoccupation with change makes them somewhat indifferent to standard practice. They are fascinated by evolution and decay. Our aim, as music professionals, is more toward the conservation of tested ways.

Returning to the phonemes, individual sounds in any language can vary in length, in loudness, in timbre (or vocal color), and in pitch. Variations of pitch, the up-and-downness of a phrase or word-grouping, we may call cadence. European languages do not consider cadence a fixed pattern. Chinese does. A classmate of this writer, living in China, boasted of having undergone a nose-and-throat operation merely to facilitate pronunciation of the highest (is it the fourth or fifth?) of the Chinese nasals.

Cadences in English, though they may tend toward the conventional in local usage, are not fixed by custom. On the contrary, they are free and often quite fanciful. In German they can be even more so. One remembers a waiter offering a second serving, "Wünchen Sie auch Fisch?," as if it were fresh water to the dying. Also note the exaggerated, indeed almost comical risings and fallings of the voice of Arnold Schönberg's German cantata *Pierrot lunaire*.

English and American, of course, show many differences of cadence, as in the familiar "I say," and "Are you there?"

In Continental European music generally, cadence, being a free element, becomes for melody a source of illustration, as well as of emotional intensities.

To remind us of how vivid the sound-pictures can be let us recall Brahms's song about a blacksmith, "Der Schmied," in which the subject is evoked by both the vocal line and its piano accompaniment.

Brahms, "Der Schmied," op. 19, no. 4

Also Richard Wagner's exultant cry of the Valkyries as they gallop through the air on horseback, carrying to Valhalla some slain hero.

Wagner, Die Walküre, *act 3*

Helmwige's voice (at the back) through a speaking trumpet

Henry Purcell's Englishman is even more specific about attempting "from love's sickness to fly-y-y."

Purcell, The Indian Queen

A FORMAL INTRODUCTION TO THE SUBJECT

And similarly for Franz Schubert's jumping trout.

Schubert, "Die Forelle"

But the most elaborate of all such descriptions is the tenor solo which opens Handel's *Messiah,* where the most expert (by far) of England's vocal composers (a foreigner too he was, north German by way of Italy) offers a musical idea so bold as to be almost a caricature of its text. Coloratura for the male voice seems neither to have fazed him nor shocked the faithful, when he depicted Isaiah's promise to flatten out the earth in order to "make straight in the desert a highway for our God."

Handel, Messiah

A FORMAL INTRODUCTION TO THE SUBJECT

Stresses, in English, are not free at all; they are fixed for both speech and singing. You cannot with impunity change the tonic accents of English words or word-groups, because if you do you change the meaning.

When Macbeth, about to commit a regicide, seems to hesitate, his wife cries, "Give me the knife!" Now every actress must have decided in advance which word in that exclamation to emphasize, *give* or *me* or *knife,* because in her choice lies the possibility of three distinct meanings.

On the other hand, if you pronounce Pepsi-Cola as Pepsicola, you make it meaningless in English, though it can sound convincing, if still meaningless, as possibly an Italian word.

In English the length of sounds, especially for singing, is more variable than their stressings. Their length can vary from very short to very long. Church chanting shows this variability in its simplest form:

"O come, let us sing unto the Lord; let us heartily rejoice in the strength of our salvation."

A FORMAL INTRODUCTION TO THE SUBJECT

This is a series of word-groups, none of them extensible in the context. The whole last line (to "salvation") goes best in patter.

Latin lends itself to melisma (or florid vocalizing), English to patter, French to syllabic individualization.*

Massenet, Manon

As a reminder that the art of putting English to music is largely a matter of not disturbing the fixed elements, let me repeat that the attributes of speech-sound are: stress, or accentuation, which in English is unvariable; cadence, which is extremely variable—but only within the limits of the third attribute, quantity, since certain sounds are considered extensible and others not. Accents in English cannot be changed without changing the meaning. Cadence can be widely varied to illustrate meanings or to intensify them, but only where the phonemes, or units of speech-sound, are in themselves extensible.

Mozart, Exultate jubilate

Let us examine these extensibilities a little, beginning with the consonants. For indeed consonants do vary in length, from the instantaneous *p* and *t* to the infinitely extensible *l* and *m,* which can last till breath gives out.

---

*The standard practice in setting French is one note per syllable. This makes a whole syllable out of every mute *e*. Omitting a mute *e* makes the style colloquial (as in *Madam'* or *M'sieur*). Also, a florid musical style can use slurred vowels. But the standard practice of one-note-per-syllable is what gives to French vocal music the air of being all recitative.

Undue prolongation of these is not, let me remind you, good style in art singing, though the popular canon encourages it.

Vowels are much simpler, because none is instantaneous. They are commonly classed for timbre as open, closed, or nasal; for duration as long or short. Their lengths give little trouble so long as one allows a bit of time for the long ones and does not expect the short ones to be held. *Home* is a long word; one can make it quite long but not really short, because both its vowel and its final consonant invite holding. *Pit* is a completely short word; it cannot be extended at all and understood. Two short consonants here cut off at both ends a vowel already short.

All vowels, even the shortest, are variable for length, because the consonants that surround them control their extensibility. Let us observe what the longer consonants can do to short vowel sounds, and vice versa.

There are lengthened short vowels, for instance, in *rest* and *love*. These are extended by the consonants that frame them. But the same vowels as those in *rest* and *love* are radically shortened by their consonants in *pet* and *putt*.

Then there are shortened long vowels, as in *pope* and *gate*. These same vowels *o* and *a* need more time in *home* and *lane*. The long consonants *h, m, l,* and *n* stretch them out.

Along with our vowels we must include the diphthongs and the mutes. A diphthong is two or more vowels heard in succession, such as *eye* and *you*. Mutes are decayed vowels, such as the *a* in *sofa,* and they all sound alike.

Diphthongs in English are numerous, though less so, I think, than in Russian or Portuguese. They include the so-called vowels *i* and *u*, but not the merely apparent diphthongs spelled *aw* or *ou*, whenever these are pronounced as simple vowels, as in *thaw* and *through*. Certain consonants also have a vowel behavior. The written letter *r*, for instance, except when it occurs at the beginning of a word, as in *rapid*, or between two vowels, as in *arrange*, or in combination with a short consonant, as in *betray*, is very likely to behave as if it were a vowel. It combines, for instance, with all the vowels, as in *ar, er, ir, or, ur*. In *York*, it almost makes a diphthong of the *aw* sound; in *Jersey*, it becomes the French vowel *eu*. The exact extensibility for singing of these *r* vowels is uncertain, but in general they seem to have the same minimum length as the long vowels. At the end of a word, however, they approach the brevity of a mute like the *a* in *sofa*—as in *builder, contractor, driver, passenger, motor*, and *river*. They are not true mutes, however, because for singing some can be extended, as in *S'wanee River*.

A FORMAL INTRODUCTION TO THE SUBJECT

Way down up-on de Swan-ee rib-ber,

Foster, Old Folks at Home (S'wanee River)

Singing will always show up vowel decay. The *e* sounds in *angels* and *roses,* for instance, cannot be treated as *eh,* nor yet as *uh*. A bit of the French *eu* will serve well here. The first syllable of *Jerusalem,* on the other hand, is customarily sung in the best English choirs as Juh, lengthened by a fairly open mouth. In all three cases it helps to push the lips forward just a bit. None of them is a pure vowel any longer, but neither are they quite yet fully decayed into mutes.

A mute is the shortest vowel sound possible. It has no color—and no extension. No matter how you spell it, it sounds like *uh*. French is full of mutes, as in the first syllable of *besoin* or the last one of *père*. So is German.* The mutes in English are troublesome to unmask, since many of them, though spoken, are rarely sung, for example *heav'n, sev'n, elev'n*. The final syllable here, unlike the final *a* of *sofa* or of *banana,* should not be extended at all in singing. This last word seems to have one elision, one mute, and only one proper vowel, that being of medium length, not indefinitely extensible. It could be written *b'nanuh*. The English poets, as Edgar Allan Poe pointed out, have all treated *sev'n* as one syllable.

Scissors resembles *river*. The vowels are the same, one short, with accent, and one long. Three sibilant consonants do, however, tend to tighten the rhythm of *scissors* and to speed it up.

And so, to repeat about English quantities, or durations, before returning to the stresses. All phonemes have some duration, and consonants are as

---

*In German the mute is called a *Schwa,* and it is pronounced, since classical German observes no elisions. Nor liaisons either, even in compound words, where only a slight hesitation separates the elements—two consonants in the case of *Konzertstück* (or concerto), a vowel requiring a stroke of the glottis in *Liederabend* (or song recital), and especially in compounds where the vowel itself is double, as in *Goetheabend* (or Goethe evening). Omission of the schwa can occur occasionally, but only on a very short note or in pop songs, never in speech. The very common term *heute Abend* (this evening), and there are many like it, is not a compound at all but a word-group which behaves like a compound.

variable in this respect as vowels. The only reason I do not treat them in detail is simply that though certain of these are indefinitely extensible, say *l* and *m,* the present conventions governing art music and its rendering do not admit their undue prolongation, even for expressive purposes. The vowel sounds in such music are, on the other hand, on account of their extensibility, the carriers of the free (or expressive) element in song, the up-and-downness of a melody, which I call cadence. The mutes and the short vowels, which are mostly not extensible, contribute more vigorously to the rhythmic design of a tune than to its shape. The long vowels and the diphthongs are all extensible, though not equally so, because the surrounding consonants have an effect on vowel lengths, as do also the conventional stresses in words and in word-groups-that-operate-as-words.

The word-group "How do you do?" contains two diphthongs and two long vowels. Though all of its sounds are theoretically extensible, only the final syllable *oo* can be held, and that not much. In fact, under heavy usage the other vowels tend to disappear, leaving only one true vowel and one mute, as in *H'do.*

Let us turn now to the stresses. Tonic accents in English are fixed. There are a few exceptions, such as gladiolus versus (in American) gladiolus and our library versus the English library. But such variants only call attention to the fact that English words normally admit no uncertainty about stress. Our language has many worrisome quantities (as in *scissors* and *banana*) but its stresses are firm.

French is just the other way. Its quantities are exact, but its tonic stresses are almost completely displaceable. It is the freedom of the stresses in French, in fact, that has encouraged an erroneous belief that French has no tonic accents. Unusual variations of stress in French simply mark the foreigner, or the social outsider. Changing the stress does not make a passage hard to recognize, and it does not alter the meaning of a French phrase. Only a change in word order can do that, such as "Donnez-le-moi le couteau" or "Le couteau, donnez-le-moi."

In single English words or in word-groups any change in the conventional stress makes for either comedy or nonsense.

In longer word-groups, or in sentences, shifting the stress will radically alter the meaning, as in "Give me the knife!"

In brief, stresses are the firmest element in our language. That is why it is the stresses and not the quantities that we mark in scanning verse. And the composing of these for expressive purpose is an author's job, not a composer's, who can do little more, in setting a text, than to avoid the violation of an already fixed pattern. It is, in fact, the conflict between our fixed stresses and the fixed duration of the short vowels that produces in vocal music our characteristic syncopation, as in the word *river*. Note that *er*, actually the French *eu*, here acts as a long vowel.

The whole story of English prosody in music is contained in the first line of Stephen Foster's *Old Folks at Home* (*S'wanee River*). Let us pretend to compose this, and see what happens.

If we plot only the stresses, they come out exactly as in the tune.

Now let us plot the quantities. They come out almost exact, with a syncopation on *river* inevitable. The spondee (or equalization of both stress and quantity) of *S'wanee* is merely voluntary, not inevitable, since the river's real name is *Sewanee*, in three syllables. (America tends to invent spondees, in fact, as in Jap-Ann.)

Now we are free to arrange the cadence, its rise and fall, for expressivity. Treating *Sewanee* as a two-syllable spondee makes for folksy diction. The octave skip gives distance, farawayness, hence nostalgia. The rising third permits a long last syllable, which adds more nostalgia. And so we have a melodic line that consists of words *and* music, a song phrase. It is a good one too, because its elements are mated, not just living together.

Instrumental accompaniment, where that seems needed, is another problem, because it has its own laws, exactly as the building of a melody does. But also, as in the vocal part of the composition, there is a range of activity where the imagination is free to illustrate a scene or to provoke a sentiment. But there are also passages where the composer can do little more than to underline (or to contradict) a melody's harmonic implications, or to punctuate the natural breathing points of the voice-line. What I must point out about both the voice-line and whatever instrumental accompaniment the composer may add is that their composing is not wholly a matter of improvisation.

Prosodic declamation, let me insist, is a constant in mature languages, from Schütz to Schubert, say; from Rameau to Poulenc; from Byrd to Britten; from the *Prayer-Book of Edward the Sixth* to *Four Saints in Three Acts*. Accompaniments change with fashions in emotional refinement and in dissonance content, but prosodic declamation, even in the florid style, changes very little, because the language itself, once mature, changes hardly at all.

Many devices for aiding melodic invention are historic and available— the visual, the sentimental, the comic, and of course the accents of passion. Out of any of these sources a perfect song or operatic recitative may spring full-blown from the subconscious. But sometimes a composer needs to balance rival urgencies—say, the structural and the expressive. In such a case, and all art work is full of them, he may have to accept a compromise. But compromises are not what makes art beautiful. Beauty is not a product of opposing forces, which neutralize each other, but of vector forces, which combine. And the combining of words with music is a technique no less frozen and no less free than the combining of instrumental parts with one another into a harmonious or a nonharmonious counterpoint. Some of the procedure is rigid, and that makes it a technique. Some of it leaves free play to the fancy, and that makes vocal writing an art. Observing only the rigidities will not make art a communication, because there is no communication without some expressive intent. And neither will expressive intent make either art *or* communication. These can only be made by an expressive intent, conscious or unconscious, working within a framework of accepted customs.

The deliberate violation of these traffic rules is any artist's privilege, in many cases his glory. Ignorance of them, however, is no excuse for messes. There are lots of English-speaking composers on the road these days, many of them hoping to arrive at Parnassus by way of the opera, the oratorio, the vehicles of choral setting and of song. And it is terrifying to watch them break up their means of transport every time they come to a textual passage that presents anything beyond average complexity of word-groupings or of enunciation. This essay is not offered as a course in how to avoid such mishaps. There is, to my knowledge, no such course available in the English-speaking world. What *is* available is a body of surviving folk song and a repertory of vocal composition in English covering more than four centuries, in which the composer can find for himself solutions for many of the emergencies.

None of the problems is new, and a composer with an ear for his own language can solve many of them without consulting precedents. The only fatal procedure is to forget that English is one of the most varied and expressive of all languages. Attempts to write music in it, or to sing it, as if it were Italian or German or French or Russian or Yiddish (and I've heard every one of these tried) are bound to failure.

Admitting that English really exists, however, that its nature is its nature, and that its behavior under stress is no less individual than that of any other language is to put oneself in a position from which its musical employment can be seriously, even hopefully perhaps, envisaged.

CHAPTER TWO

Word-Groups

If the singing of words is to be thought of as intoned speech, which it is, then for any singer the main question is: "Who's talking?"

It is also the first decision to be made by the composer before setting a text. The assumption to be avoided in every case is that music, certainly the vocal part of it, speaks only for the composer. It is not the voice of the composer, any more than the characters in a play represent the author of it.

Impersonation is the whole of almost any dramatic situation; and it is as unavoidable in liturgical uses as it is in theaters or on the concert stage. A sacred text may offer us the voice of a Prophet, or that of worshipers met together for praises and prayers, or of a biblical narrator, or of the Holy Comforter, even of God Himself. The composer is merely a transmitter of such a message. In liturgical situations this is rarely chosen by him, though for recital songs the choice may indeed have been his own. On secular occasions the vocal line is usually the voice of a poet, even when impersonating someone else's rejoicings or laments; or he too may also be just a storyteller.

After we, the listeners, have learned who is talking, we have some right as well to know what he is talking about. And the closest we can get to that is through hearing his words. An obscure verbal text—and believe me both poets and prophets love to hide their meanings, or themselves to hide behind a mass of meanings—an obscure text is best transmitted by its own words clearly projected. Certainly any willful obscurity on the literary side is not helped by faulty enunciation. Vowels insufficiently differentiated, consonant finals omitted, and tonic accents misplaced produce a confusion that renders even the most straightforward writing inept as communication.

At this point we must remember that the cardinal difference between language sung or spoken and language written down is that the latter presents itself to the eye as a string of words separated by spaces and arranged in lines. These words are spelled out in letters that give us only their sound. The letters themselves have no meaning; they are merely signs for sound.

WORD-GROUPS

Words, translated into sounds, do have meanings, often several quite different meanings; but the transmission of thoughts or of feelings requires that the words be pronounced (or read) as word-groups. Word-groups and groups of word-groups, which are where communication begins, are not indicated in the usual layouts of written or printed language, though shorthand systems do include abbreviations for some of the commoner word-groups. Groupings must therefore be determined by the speaker or, if they are to be sung, by the composer, before they can be presented to a listener. They are the minimal transmission units of either speech or song.

Let me give a few examples. "How do you do?" is a word-group. Its constituent words, though frequently used in other groupings, here have to be said together. All word-groups behave like words, this particular group as if it were a four-syllable word with a tonic accent on the last. Any attempt to separate the syllables or to misplace the accent will produce confusion. Also, though punctuated as a question, it is never so pronounced, being simply a salutation, nothing more.

Its commonest answer, "Very well, I thank you," does tend, curiously enough, toward the rising voice. This is a two-part word-group with possible accents on *well* and *thank*. If sung as an answering recitative for two persons, it allows the accent on *thank* to be weakened just a trifle, in order to bring out the rhyme of *do* and *you*. Metrical verse, rhyming, and patter all allow distortion in word-groups, and especially in groups of word-groups.

They actually invite the imposition of rhythmic patterns on to natural speech-cadences. In English, however, the displacement of a tonic accent will almost invariably either change the meaning of anything or produce nonsense. I suggest therefore to composers preparing to set words that they line out the verbal text into word-groups and their relevant further groupings.

My first example is Milton's sonnet "On His Blindness," a poem so little oratorical and so deeply reflective that it seems scarcely suitable at all for musical setting. It could, however, be set for singing, just as it can be marked for recitation. And in either case the word-groupings would be the same.

In my analysis ⌐‾‾⌐ indicates a single word-group. For double or larger groupings I use ⌐‾‾⌐ ⌐‾‾⌐ ⌐‾‾⌐.

I include here also William Blake's "Tiger! Tiger!" and a song from Shakespeare's *Measure for Measure*. The latter lines, actually written to be sung, are so exigent musically that their grouping comes out in at least one of them, quite surprisingly, to compress the words *lips* and *away* into a unit every bit as strong as "How do you do?"

Take, O, take those lips away

Here are all three poems broken down into their constituent word-groups and groups of word-groups:

John Milton, "On His Blindness"

When I consider | how my light | is spent
E're half my days | in this dark world | and wide,
And that one Talent | which is death | to hide,
Lodg'd with me | useless, | though my Soul | more bent
To serve therewith | my Maker, | and present
My true account | lest he | returning | chide,
Doth God exact day-labour, | light deny'd,
I fondly ask; | But patience | to prevent
That murmur, | soon replies, | God doth not need
Either man's work | or his own gifts, | who best
Bear his mild yoke, | they serve him best, | his State
Is Kingly. | Thousands | at his bidding | speed
And post | o'er Land and Ocean | without rest:
They also serve | who only stand | and wait.

William Blake, "The Tiger"

Tiger! | Tiger! | burning bright
In the forests | of the night,
What immortal hand | or eye
Could frame | thy fearful symmetry?
In what distant deeps | or skies
Burnt the fire | of thine eyes?

On what wings dare he aspire?
What the hand dare seize the fire?
And what shoulder, and what art,
Could twist the sinews of thy heart?
And when the heart began to beat,
What dread hand? and what dread feet?
What the hammer? what the chain?
In what furnace was thy brain?
What the anvil? what dread grasp
Dare its deadly terrors clasp?
When the stars threw down their spears,
And water'd heav'n with their tears,
Did he smile his work to see?
Did he who made the Lamb make thee?
Tiger! Tiger! burning bright
In the forests of the night,
What immortal hand or eye,
Dare frame thy fearful symmetry?

William Shakespeare, "Take, O, Take Those Lips Away"
(a song from *Measure for Measure*)

Take, O, Take those lips away
That so sweetly were forsworn;
And those eyes, the break of day,
Lights that do mislead the morn.
But my kisses bring again, bring again,
Seals of love, but seal'd in vain, Seal'd in vain.

Please note that no single word or word-group has here any meaning save in the context. It is merely a unit for pronunciation. It cannot be interrupted, nor can its conventional accent be changed. Double or triple word-groups do allow, if the speaker or composer so chooses, a slight hesitation between the groups, though not a real pause. The natural word and word-group accents remain firm. And a meaning related to that of the sentence that encloses them has begun to appear. This cannot be complete, of course, until a verb turns up.

I suggest that beginning composers, and those whose native language is not ours, practice this analysis of texts into meaningful word-groupings as an exercise in the idomatic enunciation of English. It cannot guide their melodic invention, but it will surely help toward giving to any text its maximum of plain speaking.

Regarding common phrases as word-groups. "In a minute" is a group, just like "How do you do?" In any context it behaves like a single word and is indivisible.

"Just a minute" is not so straightforward. It can be broken apart into two elements, and accented in several different ways. Like Lady Macbeth's "Give me the knife," it can change its meaning with different stresses. It is therefore a dual group, not a single one, and must be represented as just a minute.

Single word-groups, even in nonsense poetry, remain intact unless they are subjected to distortions that result from a rigorously applied rhythmic sequence. This can produce a highly comic effect without disturbing the real identity of the words.

Gertrude Stein, "Susie Asado"

Sweet sweet sweet sweet sweet tea.
Susie Asado.
Sweet sweet sweet sweet sweet tea.
Susie Asado.
Susie Asado which is a told tray sure.
A lean on the shoe this means slips slips hers.
When the ancient light grey is clean it is yellow, it is a silver seller.
This is a please this is a please these are the saids to jelly.
These are the wets these say the sets to leave a crown to Incy.

WORD-GROUPS

Incy is short for incubus.

A pot. A pot is a beginning of a rare bit of trees. Trees tremble, the old vats are in bobbles, bobbles which shade and shove and render clean, render clean must.

Drink pups.

Drink pups drink pups lease a sash hold, see it shine and a bobolink has pins. It shows a nail.

What is a nail. A nail is unison.

Sweet sweet sweet sweet sweet tea.

The poems here marked for their constituent word-groups are all relatively familiar—one each by Milton, William Blake, and Shakespeare, and one by Gertrude Stein. I do not insist that my analysis of their multiple groupings is the only one possible, though I do think my single groups are correct. Those involving more than one do tend, in their contexts, to cohere. And there is in Blake's "Tiger!" a whole line that seems to allow no interruption when it says, " . . . and when the heart began to beat."

These layouts are not for the composer to follow literally, though no single group will permit any change of accentuation; nor can its run-through be interrupted. Also, they have little to do with expression; they are merely phonetic units that when strung out in a given order do produce a verbal discourse, and inevitably some kind of meaning.

CHAPTER THREE

Occasions for Singing

As for the kinds of music available to word setters, the choice is large and generally determined by occasions—liturgical, theatrical, social, or casual. The following are among the most common:

1. *Melodrama*—familiar with films, televison, and stage plays—is instrumental music played along with speaking, sometimes called "voice-over." Here the musical continuity must dominate, but without obscuring the words or competing with them for loudness. A flowing musical texture is likely to work best, with a minimum of counterpoint.

2. *Church chanting* is a repeating music-pattern for reciting a lengthy text. It uses a plain harmonic accompaniment, or none. Clarity has no urgency here, since the texts—psalms, prayers, and canticles—are familiar. If they are not, then a clean enunciation is needed in which crescendo, diminuendo, and rhythmic emphasis are to be avoided.

3. *Patter* is a rapid articulation of verses, usually comic and rhymed, which invites in the accompaniment both rhythmic support and comical additions.

4. *Recitative,* rhymed or unrhymed, mimics the patterns of speech. Verbal clarity is important here, and some expression may be of value. Only one person sings at a time. Accompaniments to recitative must be harmonically straightforward and as simple as possible. Rhythm, if overt, must not interfere, nor should contrapuntal interest ask for attention. A verbal text and its easy reception are the essentials.

5. *Arioso* is informal as to structure and expressive in its purpose. Less static than an aria, it is valuable for advancing the drama.

6. The *aria,* either classical or modern, is a set-piece. It explains with intensity, is an emotional outpouring or, at the least, a sustained account. Paired with a free-form recitative, it can easily last twenty minutes. It is of great value to opera or oratorio, where it can offer detailed characterization and invite extended audience enjoyment of both the story and its musical

setting. It does not advance the drama; it merely intensifies by musical means its emotional content. It can be declamatory in mood, or quiet.

7. The *duet* is an aria for two persons that can also be either declamatory (argumentative) or jointly declarative, as in love scenes. The accompaniment may be illustrative, as in the lovemaking passages from Wagner's *Tristan und Isolde,* or merely supportive, as so often with the Italian masters, even in love scenes.

8. *Concerted pieces* are static like arias. They usually mark a confrontation, as in the celebrated quartets from Verdi's *Rigoletto* and from Mozart's *Don Giovanni*. They are sustained by their musical continuities, but they also involve strong contrasts of character. Their vocal counterpoint is therefore differentiated, nonhomogeneous; also, it is generated largely by characterization. Choral additions, once identified, can enrich the literary background.

9. The *madrigal* is a vocal work for individual voices, commonly four to six, in which the counterpoint, no matter how elaborate, is homogeneous, that is to say, nondifferentiated by characterization. It is not a dramatic form, but a lyric poem or ballad set for joint performance by a small number of singers, often without accompaniment. Its relation to the verbal text is the same as that of a recital song; verbal clarity is important. Its liturgical equivalents are the choral motet (unaccompanied) and the anthem (with keyboard support).

10. Ballets can also involve some vocal presence, spoken or sung. In these works, though dancing takes first place, hearing the words is helpful.

11. In the *scena,* any opera may have a moment of pantomime along with the singing. This must, however, advance the dramatic action.

12. The most elaborate of all vocal usages is the scene- or act-finale. This summarizes the story before a pause, or terminates it. Musically and dramatically finales are free in form. They can include recitatives, solos, concerted numbers, choral comments, as well as confrontations, quarrels, surprises, discoveries, happy endings, insoluble dilemmas, and tragic outcomes. The second act finale of Mozart's *Marriage of Figaro* and the whole of Wagner's *Götterdämmerung,* which finishes off all four operas of "The Nibelung's Ring," are triumphs of musical invention without sacrifice of dramatic credibility.

Modern choral music, I may add, as we encounter it today in church services or in oratorios on sacred texts, is rarely convincing. Musically ingenious it often is, but somehow many find it hard to believe that the composer himself really trusts, deeply trusts the truth of the text he has been setting. It is rather as if all the texts, sacred as well as secular, had been approached wholly as dramatic pretexts for choral experiment.

It has long seemed strange to me that nobody has yet made an oratorio out of the Communist Manifesto of 1848 by Marx and Engels. It is a text of remarkable eloquence, and for many an article of faith proudly held.

Choral contributions to symphonic works, with or without vocal solos, are not primarily vocal music. The voice-parts in these are less important as musico-literary collaborations than as adjuncts to the orchestral writing, even when the words are by famous poets.

The concert song is a special form. In the seventeenth century it appeared in Italy and in England with high musical distinction, though the poetry used was not always of the highest quality. Then it became inactive till Schubert revived it in the early years of the nineteenth century. The experiments of Haydn, Mozart, and Beethoven toward invigorating it are negligible. Arias they could write handsomely, and did; but their simple songs, save for some ingenious accompaniments, are on the whole stiff and not very responsive to interpretation. Religion (Protestant) had brought out devotional moods and continued to do so, but secular poetry remained in all the languages of Europe far superior to its musical treatments.

With Schubert a miracle occurs. The music becomes not only of equal quality with the very best German verse but also its mate. It gets inside a poem and stays there, intertwined unforgettably, never to be thought of henceforth as not a part of the whole idea. This miracle continued to reproduce itself for the better part of a century in the songs of Schumann, Brahms, Hugo Wolf, and Mahler, before German inspiration started running thin.

Meanwhile, its musico-poetical intensity had moved into French with Fauré, Duparc, Debussy, Ravel, and Francis Poulenc. That expansion also lasted about a century, but since the death of Poulenc in 1963 it has lost vigor. Nor has anything comparable appeared elsewhere. Isolated songs of good quality have been composed in the Scandinavian countries, in Russia, occasionally in the United States and England, certainly in Brazil. But in spite of a huge production in the last three regions, there has been nothing anywhere comparable to the great lieder of Germany and France that came to life in those countries, and only those, between, say, 1810 and 1960. Is it over, this miraculous mating of lyric poetry with music? Quite possibly.

Choral writing goes on busily everywhere with great expertness, with the best intentions, and with enough good musical ideas to keep the choirs a part of the modern-music establishment. Opera writing too goes on apace, though with little sympathy, I must say, from the great houses anywhere except in France, and occasionally in England. But opera is all the same the musical domain where music's life is least nearly extinct. Symphonic composition? Dead as a doornail. Important piano works? Yes, there are many. Chamber music has still some life in it too, though not much liberty. Musical fun and games, let's face it, are today in the musical theater. And I don't mean the theater of dancing, where audiences avid for bodies pay little attention to sound. I mean the singing stage, both popular and classical. In both these domains activity is constant. Should miracles begin to happen there none need be surprised. And not just one miracle but a chain of them, a going-on phenomenon of the kind that happens somewhere in music about every half-century with seemingly no preparation, no reason for it, and no promise in it save for the fact that it does keep going on.

That I should like to see; and indeed I may see it, since it is almost the only door in classical music still ajar.

CHAPTER FOUR

Making Everything Clear

An opera may be just a string of numbers, all complete as musical forms. And the seams that hold them together can be so smooth that transitions are not perceived. Also, as in French opéras comiques or in Viennese operettas and American musicals, the songs may be interspersed with spoken dialogue and with dancing. In every case, however, the story line is dependent on music for its pacing. A verbal text needs to be heard without effort, but the continuity that controls our attention is the musical one.

Music's intrinsic devices for holding attention are harmony, counterpoint, rhythm, and melody. The first two are largely a pleasure in hearing chords and in differentiating the expressivity of intervals as they occur in melody. These constitute specifically the musical experience. Rhythm, in the harmonic context, merely marks harmonic changes. It can also help to speed up the pacing or to hold it back. Counterpoint is by its nature multiple in both melody and rhythm. Harmonically it may assume as consonant any set of intervals, and from the twelfth century to our own this assumption has changed several times. Varieties of harmonic usage, also of rhythms both plain and multiple, actually constitute a string of musical customs that we may call the history of style.

Melody changes less noticeably than the other elements, being so frequently attached to words and to what they declare. Imitations of birdsong, cries of joy and pain, descriptions of nature in all its chaos, triplets addressed to the Holy Trinity, arbitrary orderings of the chromatic scale, all these are the constants of instrumental practice.

As for the observance in vocal music of correct, or naturalistic, speech cadences, they are the very substance of vocal writing. Once established by composers for the musical handling of any language, these cadences change very slowly. As I have remarked elsewhere, from Monteverdi to Verdi, from Rameau to Ravel and Poulenc, from Schütz to Schönberg, and from Byrd to Britten, it is the instrumental textures, the accompaniments, so to speak, that constantly change fashion, actually about every fifty years.

But the relation of words to music in all of Europe's chief languages barely changes at all. Vocally Stravinsky composed for the most part in classical Russian, and Schönberg, even in the yodeling *Sprechstimme* of *Pierrot Lunaire,* changed neither the phonemes nor the stresses of High German.

Composing for the voice does follow, of course, certain practical customs. Songs for the pop trade, just like recital songs, seldom employ a wider vocal range than the eleventh, say C to F. And the spreads possible for choral singers, whether children or college students, are known to publishers. Operatic roles for large theaters have long ago assumed for vocal soloists a two-octave range and a certain amount of voice-power, enough certainly to cut through an orchestra. Operatic vocalism also tolerates the distortion of many normal procedures.

Liturgical chant in the Anglican church, a sixteenth-century replacement for Latin chanting, is clearly the model from which English theatrical recitative has developed, insofar as this exists at all, both the English theater and the American being highly resistant to it. Its comical derivative, on the other hand, known as patter, has long flourished in English, and far more becomingly than in any other European language save possibly Spanish. Italian tolerates it occasionally, German and French almost never. Patter also suits Brazilian Portuguese, as in the hundreds of songs by Heitor Villa-Lobos. It can also accommodate itself to rhythmic overlays and melodic rigamaroles. These can be either comical in effect, or so seemingly inept that they actually give a fresh dimension to more serious music.

For very serious music, like sacred oratorios and tragic operas, the commoner forms of distortion we call "the accents of passion." These serve to depict or to bring about moments of emotional intensity so extreme that they require very high notes, or very low ones, many of these to be held, or viciously spit out. Actually, distortion consists of whatever changes from the usual are needed to make vowels carry in the highest and lowest registers and also for giving the music enough time to shake up the listener, to astonish him. It does not permit, however, any displacement of the conventional accents of English speech. A verbal text may easily be repeated for clarity, but obscuring it is not good style.

Actually, good style in speech or singing is designed to minimize the variations that inevitably creep into use. Phonetic experts, the professors of linguistic history, seek out such variations, classify them regionally and sociologically, define their unstable vowels, and derive from them "laws" of linguistic evolution. Public speakers, actors, and vocalists are standardizers, seeking ever to establish a method for projecting speech and for teaching it to others, for communicating in this way to a very large number of listeners. "Good" English is no affectation; it is the most practical way there is to carry meaning to multitudes.

I therefore recommend to composers that they leave the professors of phonetics out of their calculation, because these scholars are more interested in variations from standard practice than in supporting it. Their most useful tool for us is an invention known as the International Phonetic Alphabet, which consists of easy-to-read signs for all the phonemes, or single sounds, that exist in most languages. This, combined with lessons from a good voice teacher, will serve as guides to vocal setting. And listening to fine actors and orators will provide a schooling in the use of word-groups and of their combining into meaningful phrases that are indispensable for projecting a text.

It is customary nowadays for public speakers, particularly those reading from a prepared text, to underline in their script all significant words, which is to say, those that *must* be understood, those from which the whole meaning of a sentence could in fact be comprehended, even if many a minor word should fail to reach the listener. I recommend the practice of strongly projecting all such words, and I suggest that composers place them in any vocal line well up in the middle register. In a low register they may get lost, while at the top of the voice vowels may come to be altered and consonants omitted. The upper half of the middle register is where sung words can be enunciated best. Adjusting any vocal line to this acoustical fact is not difficult, and it is bound to be rewarding to all concerned.

CHAPTER FIVE

Helping the Performers

For composers coaching singers I do not advise that they essay to give them voice lessons. "Placing" a young voice and keeping an older one "placed," not to speak of placing it all over again, so often needful after the menopause, are chores with which technicians alone are to be trusted. The following hints may be useful, however, toward helping vocalists to project an English text without injury either to that text or to the singing mechanism.

In any language consonants need time to be heard. They are heard most clearly when they anticipate slightly the musical beat or follow it. A skillful accompanist can be of great help by seeming to keep the time-count while actually accommodating its pace to the soloist's need.

Consonants need always a clean ending, a slight *uh,* to avoid their making, at that point, no sound at all. This *uh* may be weak, in the lieder style, or strong, as is required for opera houses; but it must be there. Only when a consonant, or any string of them, occurs between two vowels can that tiny grunt be omitted.

English vowels, as spoken, so often tend to become diphthongs that for singing them some correction of casual speech-ways may be needed. The Spanish, ever addicted to phonetic spelling, write *baseball* as *beisbol.* The word *meeting,* also for Spanish an adopted one, is changed to *mitin,* since that language admits neither the short *i* nor the sound of our *ng.*

English vowel distortions for singing are chiefly a matter of using the nearest equivalent in the Italian-that-vocalists-learn for any part of a syllable requiring to be held.

Short vowels, of course, cannot be held for long, nor can mute vowels like the third *a* in banana. No, nor the final short *i* in *country, sympathy, melody* and the like, in spite of its constant misuse in folkways and indeed by live composers too.

I read some years ago a book by a well-known songwriter in which the examples were from the composer's own works.* And I remember well a passage in which the word *kiss,* hard enough to sustain at any time, was supposed to be held on an F-sharp (G-clef top line), an effort which at the tempo indicated, and with a hold added, would require at least twelve seconds. This cannot be done, of course, without using a different vowel. Such violations are not merely ineptitudes of student work; they appear constantly in the music of professional composers.

A legitimate distortion is to substitute for a final *ar, er, ir, or, ur* the French vowel *eu,* as in "S'wanee Riv*er.*" This is a true vowel sound, can be held, and is not really very different from good English usage anyway. It is also more suitable for the first syllable of *Jerusalem* than *ay* or *ee,* which tend toward the comic. *Angels* and *roses* too can benefit from a bit of the *eu* coloration, produced by merely pushing the lips forward.

Two prohibitions that I find it very important to suggest are any alteration of the customary stresses in English words and word-groups, or any change in volume that might be used to produce these accents. Accents produced by a throat push, or by any semblance of *fp,* are anathema in singing. They injure the voice and are ugly anyway. A musical phrase correctly prosodized by the composer will need no gratuitous accenting by the singer. And rhythmic stressings in the music are far best left to the accompanist. My own rule is never to misplace a tonic accent and never to allow my singers to furnish one.

To articulate a highly expressive melody with rhythmic freedom, but without duplicating this freedom in the accompaniment, was recommended by Mozart. Also by Chopin, who called it *tempo rubato* (stolen time). In popular music, particularly blues and jazz, it is called "hot." Actually it is an ancient practice. The medieval precept *Psalemus metrice vel rhytmice* leaves no doubt that the difference between measure and beat was accepted as early as the tenth century. And certainly the further duality of vocal versus instrumental—*cantus atque musica*—makes clear some freedom of operation. Moreover, just listen to the recordings of all those famous vocal artists of before and after World War I. They sang legato or staccato, portamento or detached, but nary an accentual stress will you hear. That kind of thing is for the orchestra.

*Bainbridge Crist, *The Art of Setting Words to Music* (New York: Carl Fischer, 1944).

HELPING THE PERFORMERS

Among the available kinds of vocal sound, only standard European-style studio production is acceptable today in concert and in opera. Falsetto, or use of the male head-register, though occasionally still heard in France, is not generally admired elsewhere either in the theater or in concert performance.

Crooning, a sort of humming-with-the-mouth-open, is effective chiefly in radio and recordings. It can be ineffably sweet.

The "female baritone," heavily colored by "chest" as opposed to "head" or "mixed" resonance, though common in commercial entertainment, has no place in classical vocalism.

A common error of singers today is the constant use of crescendo-diminuendo (⟨ ⟩) on single notes. This seems to be due to shallow breathing; but since it is injurious to clear enunciation, I think a composer is wise to discourage it. It can sometimes be corrected courteously by asking for a more sustained melodic line, smoothing out to be achieved by singing the lower notes louder and the higher ones less loud.

In concert songs, one can ask for, and hope to hear sung, any vowel in any range and in any volume from p to f. For this accomplishment the highest and lowest notes of the vocal ranges cannot be used. They require too much vowel distortion, as do pp and ff in those same outlying regions. The concert song is a piece of poetry as well as of music, and no tampering with that equilibrium is of any help to the work.

Opera, on the other hand, and large-hall oratorio ask for extremities of range and volume, and demand in consequence greater distortions of "natural" speech and heavier emphases on "the accents of passion" than the lieder style, which is all for intimacies.

CHAPTER SIX

The Longs and Shorts in Singing

Anything can be set to music. A text may be in prose or in verse or in some style in between. It can be as informal as a conversation or as strictly set up as a creed or contract. It can also be as clear as a love-call, as obscure as the transcript of a mystical state, as abstract as an exercise for vocal practice.

If it is in any known language, it is a string of words or word-groups; and these consist of recognizable consonants and vowels. Such strings have their controls. All vowels, for instance, even those called short, are capable of some extension in singing. So indeed are certain consonants, though this extension is not often called for, excepting that of the *m* sound, as in humming. Vowel extension is strictly framed, though not limited, by the consonants which precede and end the vowel sound. Exceptions occur in words or groups that begin with a vowel or end with one. In the first case the vowel requires a glottis-stroke to get it started, as in *apple;* * in the second case it can simply be dropped half-said, as in *banana.*

In spoken English, syllabic stresses are as firmly a part of any word-group as are its vowels and consonants, and these stresses cannot be altered, as was remarked earlier, without changing the meaning of the phrase in which they occur. And the same is true for singing, though certain instrumental helps may be necessary in order to avoid making stress-accents with the voice, which are always unpleasant and possibly injurious.

Conventional patterns of versification are of three kinds—lengths, stresses, and rhymes. A pattern of lengths—or quantities, as they are called in the classroom—deals with syllables, and the vowel lengths in these are mostly controlled by consonants. English poetry actually follows quantitative patterns more often than is generally recognized, the fault being one of no-

*Bizet wrote to the librettist of *Carmen* regarding a song-lyric for that opera, "I call to your attention that in this poem of thirteen lines nine begin with a vowel."

menclature, since the so-called long vowels frequently occur in short syllables, and vice versa.

Any pattern of stresses, though more sharply observed in speech than in singing, is in music largely an illusion, enforced against the very nature of our language by compositional and vocal device. Even in speaking, stress patterns can sometimes be attentuated. Take the familiar lines that open Chaucer's *Canterbury Tales:*

> Whan that Aprille with his shoures soote
> The droughte of Marche hath percèd to the roote,
> And bathèd ev'ry veyne in swich licour
> Of which vertu engendred is the flour

This passage seems to demand no stresses anywhere, but to be merely an alternation (not quite exact) of long syllables with short ones. And as such, it invites singing, as Chaucer's verse in fact so often does.

Consistently accentual verse is rare in English, though an occasional strong accent can be valuable for literary emphasis. For example, in Shakespeare's *Measure for Measure,*

> Take, O, take those lips away

somehow makes the word *lips* both strong and important.

And in William Blake's "Tiger! Tiger!" just listen to this:

> What immortal hand or eye
> Dare frame they fearful symmetry?

For either recitation or singing, the *l* sound of *fearful* requires, in order not to disappear altogether before the *s,* a certain extension plus maybe even a short holding back to prepare for the *symmetry* idea. And these delays, followed by the false rhyme of *symmetry* with *eye,* creates a poetic effect quite tremendous.

Compared to the complexities of patterning caused by both quantitative meters and accentual, rhymes present no great problem to a composer. All the same, he should know the kinds of them and recognize them when they occur in poetry.

End-of-the-line rhyming is not hard to observe in music, nor to avoid observing. Following it strictly, of course, can generate monotony. Interior rhymes and assonances, which rarely occur as a pattern, can often be pointed up to advantage. False rhymes, in English a very strong effect, can usually be given lots of emphasis. The rhyming of words ending in a short *y,* such as *melody, sweetly,* and the like, is troublesome for a poet, but even more so for a composer. Under no circumstance, I think, can treating the *y* sound as a double *e* be condoned, though you may find an occasional precedent for it in folk music. Rhyming penultimate or antepenultimate syllables can be entertaining in comic poetry, say *bunny* with *honey,* or *funny* with *money.*

Rhymes, neither the patterned ones that appear at line-endings nor the informal ones that can turn up anywhere, need not be emphasized by the singer. Indeed, just as in recited poetry, they may well be softened a bit to avoid monotony and to carry the sentence forward. A good false rhyme, however, is likely to need some space around it to make it clear, as when in the Purcell and Dryden *King Arthur,* for instance, a hymn to the glories of England boasts of her export trade:

> Foreign lands, thy fishes tasting,
> Learn from thee luxurious fasting.

And when the pagan river-nymphs essay to tempt the good king from his chastity, it is with a false rhyme naturally.

> Come play with us an hour or two;
> What danger from a naked foe?

In patter songs, however, rhyme will be all the more welcome if you give it speed, as in Gilbert and Sullivan's *Pinafore:*

> And so do his sisters and his cousins and his aunts,
> His sisters and his cousins whom he reckons by the dozens,
> His sisters and his cousins and his aunts.

There is, as we know, a long musical history of suggesting stress-accents without using stresses. Before the invention of the orchestra, when music was still dominated by instruments incapable of stress-accents, namely the pipe organ and the harpsichord, there was simply no easy way of signaling to the listener what the meter of any piece was supposed to be. It might be duple meter or triple or even some additive string of these, such as occurs in liturgical chant or in recitative.

Before Bach one cannot be sure of exactly what happened in rendering meter, but by his time certainly a method had been established for making

THE LONGS AND SHORTS IN SINGING

the measure clear on instruments which could not play downbeats. This was a technique of composing themes, and of starting off almost any piece, with a note longer than those that follow.

Bach, Das Wohltemperirte Klavier, *book 1, fugue in c ♯*

Bach, Fugue in e for organ, "The Wedge"

Bach, Trio Sonata for Organ no. 1

Bach, Die Kunst der Fuge, *principal theme and its inversion*

Bach himself, in the forty-eight fugues of *Das Wohltemperirte Klavier,* did not always follow this recipe. He was very likely to hold our attention by beginning a fugal subject in the middle of a measure, preferably on the second count of say six, and continuing in regular eighth-notes or six-teenths until the counter-subject, by appearing clearly on a downbeat, gets us straightened out.

Nevertheless, a long first-count has remained characteristic of practically all the music of the great masters even as late as Claude Debussy and Igor Stravinsky.

A further device, still used by organists and harpsichord players, for making a long note sound like a strong note is either to hold back an imperceptible moment before sounding it or to hold on to it a similar small amount of time before continuing.

Singing, when practiced in the manner now considered classical for recitals, oratorios, and opera, no more invites the strong accents characteristic of English speech than orchestral string playing will tolerate unneeded up-bow crescendos and down-bow diminuendos, or carelessly easygoing heel-of-the-bow attacks. A sustained line at any volume in any range is the norm of musical utterance today, even for instruments of percussion. Any alteration of this for expressive purposes must be clearly intentional; otherwise it creates a misunderstanding.

Similarly, singing holds our attention best when the sound of it is a steady sound. This should be so whether the pitches are high or low, the volume loud or soft. Anything beyond this kind of vocal discipline, including the proper enunciation of words and word-groups, must be planned, laid on, an added grace, a gift to the listener. And for this the listener will surely be grateful; not as grateful perhaps as the voice lovers will be for a beautiful sound, but as grateful as any lover of fine music can be for a musicianly performance. Actually, for an artist of native powers less than those of a Flagstad or a Pavarotti, musicianship is the only way to get by.

So please, my singers, make your accents by other means than plain vocal stress. Use your consonants to delay the vowel sounds or to anticipate them. Also to close them off cleanly. Let me think you are stressing the syllables that seem to require that; but at the same time keep on pouring out sound with the steadiness of a pipe organ. That is the way Caruso worked, and Chaliapin, and Rosa Ponselle, and Schumann-Heink, and Nellie Melba, and John McCormack, and all the rest of those wonderful artists now dead but still remembered and also preserved for us in their recordings. The great ones in opera, in oratorio, in lieder, all sang like that. They enunciated too, and a few could even act. But whatever they did besides to vocalize, they did under musical controls—whether moving or miming or just standing still. And certainly, when singing both words and music, they were making music speak.

Instrumental Helps and Hindrances

In the matter of accompaniment, especially for concert songs, the same question arises as for the voice line: "Who is speaking?"

The simplest accompaniment, and by far the most effective for songs of modest pretension, is a literal doubling of the voice-line supported by plain harmonies. This gives the song a musical shape while helping to carry the tune. It is practically universal in the popular styles and by no means without value to the classical. It speaks, along with the melody itself, for the author of the words. And a bit of countermelody can sometimes add warmth.

More common among skilled composers is a contrasted accompaniment, which gives harmonic support as needed, but which at the same time depicts something. Schubert's jumping trout, anybody's running water, imitations of the Spanish guitar, of a church organ, of a marching band, of trumpet calls, all these can provide a further embellishment to the voice of the poet. By adding an almost visual evocation they add richness to the music and help to dramatize a situation.

Here are a few suggestions about the various kinds of music that can be used as contrasting accompaniments.

1. With triadic harmonies I advise keeping the accompaniment harmonically complete; don't expect the singer to help you define a chord. Seventh-chord harmonies must also be fully expressed. With harmonies still more complex a great deal of hidden note-cueing will be needed for safety.

2. If a countermelody is used, be sure the listener can recognize its identity and purpose. Who is it that is singing along with our soloist and what is he saying?

Also, the voice, though it may seem independent of the countermelody, is pretty sure to need some helping out from discreetly placed cue-tones.

3. Do not change the identity of the contrasting music without making clear what is taking place. Background music can represent people (crowds

and choruses), or machines (industrial noises), or animals (say birds). Or it may be a voice of nature, like running water or rustling leaves. It can give us explosions too, with maybe some fire. Rain and wind are easy, storms quite common. Cats are easier than dogs. Horses in motion are no trouble at all. Rocks, mountains, things that neither move nor make a noise are very hard to evoke. In general it is unwise to try evoking more than one kind of thing at a time, or even in the same piece.

4. In opera, themes that characterize people are a heritage often credited to Wagner. Mozart used dance-meters to define social class—minuets for the upper, country dances for peasants. All such signals can be counterpointed for dramatic complexity and they can be just as distinctive as *Leitmotive* in a concerted number or an act-finale.

Bach regularly illustrated the about-to-be-sung words in his chorale preludes for organ, sometimes with almost comic effect, as when angels trip down from heaven, or when Adam's fall from grace is pictured by a descending major seventh on the pedals.

The most entertaining of all these antics are Handel's detailed uses in the *Messiah* of the vocal line itself to picture valleys being "exalted" and "rough places plain," as well as "people that wander" chromatically "in darkness" all round the minor mode, until suddenly, in steadier pitches, they "have seen a great light."

5. Musical illustration has long used earlier musical styles to evoke periods of history. The medieval and baroque are easy to characterize, classical Greece and Rome much harder. Places such as Spain, Scotland, India, and Japan can be situated through instrumental textures such as guitars, bagpipes, and stringed instruments plucked, or through their vocal folklore. Even in the United States musical styles are used to suggest class—jazz or gospel for blacks, commercial pop for the middle classes or for youth, showtunes by Cole Porter, Gershwin, and the like for a country-club world.

6. A very old convention is to use against a free melodic line an accompaniment made wholly of abstractions. The most familiar of these is the oom-pah, of which there is, I must say, a surprising amount in Beethoven's *Fidelio*. But no less abstract are scales, arpeggios, and repeating rhythms. These can be compared in our own time to the squares, circles, and discs found regularly in the paintings of Joan Miró and the sculptures of Alexander Calder. They are as modern as anything could be and also as ancient as the egg-and-dart pattern or the Greek key. I recommend them highly, and

suggest further that they can be employed very effectively with off-key harmonies and contradictory rhythms. Dissonant intervals, after all, are not the only form of modernism. Multiplicities, contradictions, contrasts, and distortions are no less valuable.

May I add that polymetrics and polyharmony, delightful as they are, need special handling. Rhythmic independence in the accompaniment is also welcome if the voice-line is simple. If not, it may interfere with projecting the words.

Multiple harmonies may interfere with the voice-line unless the latter can be recognized as belonging to one of the harmonic lines. For these latter I recommend using only common chords—major and minor triads, the diminished seventh, dominant seventh, or any grouping of tones from the six-tone scale. Such chords must be heard in close position, and contrasted to one another in timbre, in height, and, when practical, in volume. Harmonic lines may be counterpointed against one another, but not within a chord, as by suspensions. By keeping all harmonic identities recognizable and separate, you will be rewarded with a "musical" effect, an on-pitch blend of instrumental sound that sets off most surprisingly the vocal. Be careful in all this to keep the volume down. And remember the accompaniment's identity, who or what it purports to represent by being the way it is.

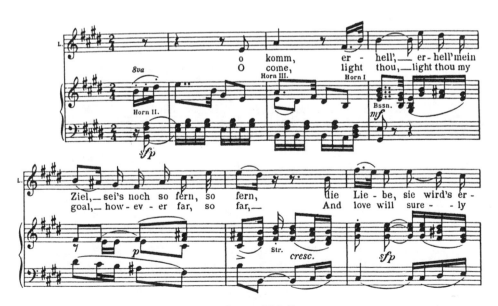

Beethoven, Fidelio

INSTRUMENTAL HELPS AND HINDRANCES

Vocally a showpiece for dramatic soprano with a full two-octave range (B–B).

The accompaniment doubles, or almost, the voice-line, a wise procedure when the singer is on stage and the orchestra half buried in a pit.

The orchestra also gives us, often right along with the melody itself,

INSTRUMENTAL HELPS AND HINDRANCES

richly harmonized, almost every accompaniment formula known to music. These include broken chords, arpeggios, bits of oom-pah, repeated notes, ejaculated chords, syncopated chords, tremolando sostenuto, martellato, or agitato, and scales both smooth and jerky. The purpose of all this variation seems to be holding the listener in a state of anxiety while building for the singer a series of climaxes.

The aria, though structured by a master musician, contains far more excitement than drama, a situation that tends to characterize the whole opera.

Falla, Siete canciones populares españolas, *no. 2,* Seguidilla murciana

INSTRUMENTAL HELPS AND HINDRANCES

Here we have Spanish so rapid that it approaches patter and a characteristic Spanish cantilena rhythmically controlled. The control is a guitar initiation that supports the dance-pattern, a seguidilla.

The poem is a version of the proverb which advises those who live in glass houses not to throw stones.

CHAPTER EIGHT

The "Musical Idea"

Suppose we are about to write a piece for singing. Suppose also that we know the kind of public usage that piece will have—in church, say, or recital, concert, light theatricals, as incidental music in a play or film, an aria in some work for choir and orchestra, or a major position in an opera. Next we need to know what the verbal text is. Now how do we get started on the music?

Some composers first look toward finding for the words a suitable rhythm. This approach to melody is, I think, largely American. Europeans are more likely to think in tones and to lay on metrics afterward. Their shaping of the tune can follow any number of patterns remembered from music's history.

The oldest of these is essentially vocal, derived from the plainchant and constructed out of the tetrachords that define the church modes. Writers as modern as Debussy, Stravinsky, and Arnold Schönberg have often used these modes for a source. And practically every composer since Mozart has used arpeggios.

Many composers find a harmony first, then let the melody cover its constituent tones. This is ancient practice, being derived from the imitation of trumpets and hunting-horns, for which an arpeggio is actually the scale of the instrument. French folk songs, many very old indeed, are virtually all of them either horn-calls, or else they are modal tetrachords fitted to language. In modern times too, both soldiers and sailors have tended to set their bugle-calls to words.

Horn-call melody, old French

Beethoven, Symphony no. 3, horn-call theme

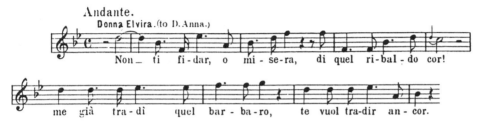

This is almost a horn melody. Only the A's are not quite in tune.
Mozart, Don Giovanni

Imitating a vocal style for performing instrumental music, "making it sing," is constantly being recommended to us. But the evocation of instruments by the singing voice is no less familiar. Sopranos pretending to be flutes, mezzos as clarinet or English horn, are thoroughly effective. And writing in the florid bassoon style for a bass soloist was for Handel ever a jolly game. So also, for many another composer of the eighteenth century, was asking his chorus to work in disjointed syllables, for all the world as if they were an orchestra of bowed strings.

And there is a shivering chorus in Purcell's *King Arthur* that I find strange. I am not at all sure how these repeated notes should be sung.

Purcell, King Arthur

THE "MUSICAL IDEA"

We may assume, I suppose, that a choir can do whatever any singer can, though the extremes of operatic range may be ill advised, as indeed they are too for many a soloist. There is little difference between solo writing and the choral possibilities, though individual characterization of persons is not common in group work. A chorus can easily sing like an assembly of soldiers, of course, or angels, or union members, or simply friends and neighbors. And in Russian operas they quite regularly, since Mussorgsky, represent the soul of the Russian people.

In every case, of course, vocal music, whether for soloists, concerted groups, madrigalists, or massed forces, has to have some kind of a tune; and the tune must fit the words. The tune can come from anywhere—from church chant, folk song, or instrumental imitation. It can make like marching armies, crowds in chaos, or women at their household chores, but only rarely like single characters declaring their feelings or their future intentions. *I* and *me* are a bit more convincing in the madrigal style, particularly when individual voices are contrasted.

How does a tune, or melody, come about? How is it made? My analysis of its elements, its materials, goes rather like this. Its smallest fragment, like a word-group in spoken language, is generally called a motif. This has tones chosen from a modal tetrachord, a scale, or an arpeggio. Let me cite the motif that starts off Beethoven's Fifth Symphony, which has both a tonal shape (two descending thirds, one major and one minor, make up the tetrachord) and a meter (da-da-da-daaah twice).

Beethoven, Symphony no. 5

The first line of the *Dies Irae,* on the other hand, though clearly a modal tetrachord, is rhythmically indeterminate.

Thomas of Celano, Dies Irae

When you enlarge a motif and vary it, say you lengthen it to present an antecedent and a consequent, you have a musical phrase, but still not a melody. Just running on is not melody either. We call that melopoeia.

A formal melody may be short, but it is likely to include at least three full phrases, which can be heard as a beginning phrase, a middle one, and some kind of a final one, an ending. When Saint-Saëns gave pupils his famous assignment, "Bring me eight measures that I can play without accompaniment," he was asking for a complete musical statement, long enough to have three recognizable sections and plain enough to need no booster from chordal harmony.

I know that adding harmony to everything can be a temptation, because chords are music's chief intoxicant. They are what sends chills up your spine, not melody nor counterpoint nor rhythm. But chords, whether in sequence or casual, are only one of music's materials, and omitting them is one of the disciplines in learning to compose.

Now I come to the really indispensible chip in creating music, which I am calling here the "musical idea." And a musical idea, just like any other kind of idea, can be either fresh or stale, but it must be about something; it is an object with two aspects, like a coin.

A melody joined to a harmony, or contrasted with one, can constitute a musical idea; and so can a song with accompaniment. The song itself in that case, its own words and melody, are also a musical idea, perhaps even a full statement of one.

Any duality, of course, any mixture of musical elements, is no better than the materials that went into it. A simple oom-pah bass with a country fiddle can work beautifully when both are straightforward, authentic. A slightly more uncommon contrast, say a rhythm of three-against-four, can excite the attention of musical sophisticates, though since Brahms it is no great novelty. A bigger surprise comes in Rimsky-Korsakov's *Spanish Caprice* where he accompanies a violin cadenza with snare-drum rolls. Any suddenly encountered strangeness in the contrast can delight a musical mind. It can also deeply shock one less open to the unfamiliar. Actually the introduction of surprise rhythms, along with strident orchestral sonorities and less-than-suave harmony, are the circumstance that has produced the unmistakably "antimodern" musical reaction now common for well over a century. All musical ideas, I know, are not necessarily good ones. But you cannot write music without a musical idea. The best of these do involve, have always involved, even the oldest ones around, some still refreshing surprise. And the quality of authenticity, of a no-nonsense approach to music, is often the biggest surprise of all.

To repeat. You cannot write music without a musical idea, but a musical idea is not a composition. An extension of the idea into a three-part statement is composition. And the further extension of this statement through repetition, variation, and contrast can make a composition of some amplitude. The amplitude may tend toward an emotional pattern of anxiety-and-relief. It can also make, through auditory imitations and rhythmic recalls (especially of motion), suggestions of the visual or the kinetic, as well as reminders of other musical sounds, many kinds of them. In every case the overall patterning and the timing of its reception by the human body are musical. Even a piece with words to it, a vocal work composed for singing, makes its continuity and its climax, if there is to be one, through devices specifically musical.

The words are always there, of course; and they do create a metrical pattern of phonemes. This is a vocal work's only instrinsic continuity. Emotionally and factually they may seem to be telling their own story, but in reality they are doing very little more than to explain the music. By the very nature of musical reception, its unbelievable speed and intensity as compared to language, a piece of vocal music is primarily music. The words are received much more slowly, and they may even be in a foreign language. No wonder they must be set with precision, articulated with love, and projected with a constant care. They are related to the musical idea that frames and explains them, but they are themselves no part of it. Giving to the listener an illusion that they are really needed for full enjoyment is a triumph of certain great musical artists. Others get by, especially singing high and loud, with little effort toward anything more; and these are as often as not the artists whom voice lovers reward.

CHAPTER NINE

Both Words and Emotions Are Important

When I began in the early 1920s to compose music for texts by Gertrude Stein, my main purpose was musical. Or let us say musical and linguistic. For the tonal art is forever bound up with language, even though a brief separation does sometimes take place in the higher civilizations, rather in the way that the visual arts will occasionally abandon, or pretend to abandon, illustration. The musical art, moreover, in its more ambitious efforts toward linguistic union, has regularly entwined itself with liturgical texts and dramatic continuities.

Now the liturgical connection has been operating successfully ever since medieval times and even earlier; but in Western Europe it regularly had bypassed the local dialects and the budding languages, remaining attached for administrative reasons to the formalistic, the far less vivid Latin. The first modern tongues to take on music liturgically (the first gesture after their doctrinal breakaways from Rome) were English and German, both in the sixteenth century. The Latin-based local idioms had made no great effort toward entering the Catholic liturgy until today's ecumenical trend got them involved. But toward the end of that same sixteenth century, which was producing liturgically such remarkable results for English and for German, Italian musicians in Florence had begun to perfect for secular purposes (for the stage) a blending of music with language so miraculously homogenized that a new word had to be found for it. They called it *opera*, or "work"; and work was actually what it did, invigorating the theater internationally in a manner most remarkable. For the English poetic theater, after the times of Elizabeth I and James I, began to lose vigor at home and never seemed able to travel much abroad. But the Italian lyric theater in less than a century had begun to implant itself in one country after another and in one language after another. Born around 1580 as tragedy to be sung throughout (which is its profound originality and from birth its unshakable integrity), opera took on French with Lully in the middle seventeenth century, German in the late eighteenth with Mozart, Russian in the nineteenth, beginning in the 1840s with Glinka.*

Serious opera seems never to have felt quite comfortable, however, in English or in Spanish, languages of which the poetic style, highly florid, made music for the tragic theater almost unnecessary. Comedies with added song and dance numbers existed of course everywhere; but music rarely served in them for much more than sentiment, being too slow, hence too clumsy a medium for putting over either sight gags or verbal jokes, except in patter songs.

Nevertheless, English-language composers have never stopped making passes at the opera. It is as if we bore it, all of us, an unrequited love. My own hope toward its capture was to bypass wherever possible the congealments of Italian, French, German, and Russian acting styles, all those ways and gestures so brilliantly based on the very prosody and sound of their poetry. For an American to aspire toward avoiding these may have seemed overambitious. But for one living in Europe, as I did for several decades, it may have been an advantage being able finally to recognize the foreignness of all such conventions and to reject them as too hopelessly, too indissolubly Italian or French or German or Russian, or even English, should some inopportune British mannerism make them seem laughable to us.

Curiously enough, British and American ways in both speech and movement differ far less on the stage, especially when set to music, than they do in civil life. Nevertheless, there is every difference imaginable between the cadences and contradictions of Gertrude Stein, her subtle syntaxes and maybe stammerings, and those of practically any other author, American or English. More than that, the wit, her seemingly endless runnings-on, can add up to a quite impressive obscurity. And this, moreover, is made out of real English words, each of them having a weight, a history, a meaning, and a place in the dictionary.

---

*The Florentine group (or Camerata) had begun with Greek music studies by Vincenzo Galilei. Giulio Caccini's *Euridice* dates from 1600. Monteverdi's *Orfeo* was produced in Mantua, 1607; but his later works were mostly performed in Venice.
The latter city is said to have supported at one time in the eighteenth century seventy-five neighborhood theaters all giving opera.

The whole setup of her writing, from the time I first encountered it back in 1919, in a book called *Tender Buttons,* was to me both exciting and disturbing. Also, as it turned out, valuable. For with meanings jumbled and syntax violated, but with the words themselves all the more shockingly present, I could put those texts to music with a minimum of temptation toward the emotional conventions, spend my whole effort on the rhythm of the language, and its specific Anglo-American sound, adding shape, where that seemed to be needed, and it usually was, from music's own devices.

I had begun doing this in 1923, before I ever met Miss Stein; and I ended it all by setting our second opera, *The Mother of Us All,* in the year of her death, 1946. This was actually her last completed piece of writing, and like our earlier operatic collaboration *Four Saints in Three Acts,* from 1927, had been handmade for me.

Four Saints is a text of great obscurity. Even so, when mated to music, it works. Our next opera, separated from the other by nineteen years and by a gradual return on her part to telling a story straight, was for the most part clear.

Both *Four Saints* and *The Mother* offer protagonists not young, not old, but domineeringly female—Saint Theresa of Avila and Susan B. Anthony. In both cases, too, the scene is historical; and the literary form is closer to that of an Elizabethan masque than to a continuous dramatic narrative. But there the resemblance ends. The background of the first is Catholic, Counter-Reformational, baroque, ecstatic. The other deals with nineteenth-century America—which is populist, idealist, Protestant, neighborly (in spite of the Civil War), and optimistic. The saints are dominated by inspirations from on high, by chants and miracles, by orders and commands, and by the disciplines of choral singing. The Americans of *The Mother,* group-controlled not by command but by their own spontaneity, are addicted to gospel hymns, darn-fool ditties, inspirational oratory, and parades. Nevertheless the music of the work, or so Carl Van Vechten found, is an apotheosis of the military march.

I do not know that this is true. All I know is that having previously set a text of great obscurity, I took on with no less joy the setting of one so intensely full of meanings, at least for any American, that it has never failed at the end to draw tears.

For this result, my having earlier worked on texts without much overt meaning had been of value. It had forced me to hear the sounds that the

American language really makes when sung, and to eliminate all those re-courses to European emotions that are automatically brought forth when European musicians get involved with dramatic poetry, with the stage. European historic models, music's old masters, are not easy to escape from. And if any such evasion, however minor, takes place in *The Mother,* that is due, I think, to both Miss Stein and myself having for so long, in our work, avoided customary ways and attitudes that when we got round to embracing them we could do so with a certain freshness.

CHAPTER TEN

Opera in the Vernacular

Opera and oratorio are made up of two kinds of writing. One is used for set-pieces, which communicate emotion; the other for conversations, which communicate facts. And though many composers, notably Richard Wagner, have aimed to make the two styles seem one, the fact remains that no matter how carefully the seams are concealed the two are not of the same stuff. And both are necessary to a musico-dramatic narrative.

A set-piece can sometimes get by with incorrect (that is, unclear) communication of words. But explanations have to be understood. Recitative must therefore either be spoken, which is not always appropriate if the subject is a noble one, or set to music by a skilled workman. The mark indeed of a dramatic master is far less his ingenuity in writing set-pieces than the way he handles his recitatives. As high points of accurate and expressive writing in this style I should like to recall here the German recitatives in Bach's *Saint Matthew Passion,* the Italian ones in Mozart's *Don Giovanni* and in Rossini's *Barber of Seville.* Musical conversation of high quality in a more modern manner exists in the first act of Wagner's *Walküre,* also in Debussy's *Pelléas et Mélisande* and in Erik Satie's *Socrate.*

No translation of vocal music, particularly of recitative, is ever quite first-class. Making the quantities, the stresses, *and* the expressive design of a good words-and-music marriage all come out convincing in a foreign language is virtually impossible. That is why translated opera is occasionally so shocking. And yet the kind of understanding in the theater that is only possible in one's own language is desirable. Germany, France, and Italy sing practically all foreign operas in their own languages.* England, the United

---

*Information from Craig Rutenberg, répétiteur at New York's Metropolitan Opera, states that the principal houses of Berlin, Hamburg, Munich, and usually Düsseldorf now use the original languages, while the regional houses, even Stuttgart, tend to sing only in German. In France, he adds, the provincial houses still use translations, with only Paris and Lyon singing operas consistently in their original languages. (Before the last war such a procedure was far from consistent.)

States, Spain, Portugal, and the Latin American countries tend to use, where possible, the original languages. Formerly opera in Russia was polyglot, just as here. The Soviets now use mostly Russian.

It is exactly the countries that have long produced original operas in their own language—Italy, France, Germany, Russia, the countries where opera has taken root—that are the least bothered by translation's inefficiencies. I think this is due to the existence there of a large body of work well written for the local tongue. When the basic repertory has something that gives everyone pleasure (and there is no greater pleasure in music than hearing one's own language vocalized), it becomes unthinkable to deny anyone that pleasure, even though the degree of the pleasure, in foreign works, is far from complete.

But even where there is no such basic local repertory, audiences do not always feel happy about translations. They want to feel that somewhere in the opera deal they are getting something authentic, even though this may involve the sacrifice of comprehensibility. Germany had Italian opera always, until first Mozart wrote two and Beethoven one and then Weber about eleven operas in correctly prosodized German. After 1815, there was a real German repertory, and all the foreign operas were translated into German, and it never again occurred to anybody in Germany or Austria that German was not the most appropriate language in the world for singing, including the performance of foreign operas.

Here in the United States we are not quite ready for such a transition, though supertitles flashed on a screen are beginning to help. There are already a few operas well written in the English language—Gershwin's *Porgy and Bess,* perhaps; Hall Johnson's dramatic oratorio *Green Pastures;* Marc Blitzstein's *Cradle Will Rock;* Gian Carlo Menotti's *Medium* and *Consul;* my own *Four Saints in Three Acts* and *Mother of Us All,* just possibly my *Lord Byron,* not to mention the whole rich catalogue of Benjamin Britten. But all these operas still do not make up a repertory. When there are a dozen more, opera in English will cease to be a cause; it will be a fact. And reformers will then be agitating to keep foreign works in their original languages, instead of to get them out of these. What we need now is simply more operas written in English that sounds like English, put to music in such a way that there is no mistaking what language is being sung and what the words being sung are. In other words, we shall find foreign opera satisfactory in English when we shall have a repertory of a dozen or more successful operas composed in English. At that time we shall also train our singing actors primarily to work in their own language, because that will be the language that our basic opera repertory will have been composed in.

CHAPTER ELEVEN

The Nature of Opera

Let me begin my finale by talking about anyone, particularly a composer, feeling at home in theaters, having stage-sense. In France they call it *le sens du théâtre*. In any language it means an awareness of the fact that in show business—any kind of it—there is a show and there is an audience. It takes two to play theater.

Historically speaking, not all the great poets have been gifted for the stage. Shakespeare, Ben Jonson, Marlowe, Ford, and Dryden all were. Milton was not. Nor were the Romantics—Byron, Shelley, Keats, and Coleridge. Any more than were all those novelists and storytellers, from Sterne through Dickens and on to Henry James, Proust, and Joyce.

George Frideric Handel was thoroughly a stage man. Johann Sebastian Bach was not, though his *Saint Matthew Passion,* with its moving recitatives for Jesus, its terrifying crowd scenes, and its audience-participation hymns, approaches the dramatic oratorio. Mozart had an enormous stage gift; Haydn a very small one, in spite of his fifteen operas; Beethoven almost none, though he aspired to it. But Weber was wise in the theater, and Wagner virtually infallible.

What is this mysterious talent that seems to have skipped half the population? It shows up in children as impersonation, or as simply showing off, in the manipulating of family and friends through charm, later as a form of adolescent sex appeal in mimicking movie actors. And wherever the stage-sense is true, it is accompanied by an instinct for timing. In playing comedy, as in telling a joke, timing is almost the whole trick. Tragedy, sob stories, and soap opera require a less wary trajectory. Just keep them going; eventually tears will flow.

Composers of our own century have often worked well for the stage. Richard Strauss wrote upwards of ten successful operas; Debussy with *Pelléas et Mélisande* wrote only one, though there are also two fine ballets, *Khamma* and *Jeux,* as well as a pair of dramatic oratorios, *The Prodigal Son* and *The Martyrdom of Saint Sebastian*. Stravinsky's *Fire Bird, Petrouchka,* and *Rite of Spring,* to mention only his early ballets, are tops in their field, while *Les Noces* (in Russian), *Perséphone* (in French), and *Oedipus Rex* (in Latin) are first-class ballet-cantatas. There are also two far-from-negligible Stravinsky operas, relatively early *The Nightingale* (in Russian) and quite late *The Rake's Progress* (in English). Alban Berg's *Wozzeck* and his uncompleted *Lulu* are modernistic adaptations of German literary classics. Ravel, in France, wrote two successful operas, *L'Heure espagnole* ("On Spanish Time") and *L'Enfant et les sortilèges* ("The Spellbound Child"), as well as one world-famous ballet score, *Daphnis et Chloé*. The French composers of our time have in fact, like their predecessors, virtually all composed for both the singing and the dancing stage. Hence the abundant theatrical production of Milhaud, Honegger, Sauguet, and Poulenc. While in England Benjamin Britten, and in Russia Shostakovich, Prokofiev, and others have produced both operas and ballets with stage-quality.

If modern poets—Rimbaud, Valéry, Yeats, Rilke, Pound, and the surrealists—have written more often for readers than for actors, T. S. Eliot did compose four thoroughly practical plays and Gertrude Stein, in addition to quite a lot of texts that she called plays (and which have indeed been staged), was the author, along with the ballet-with-words *A Birthday Bouquet,* of two genuinely effective opera librettos—*Four Saints in Three Acts* and *The Mother of Us All,* plus just possibly *Doctor Faustus Lights the Lights*.

In Germany, Russia, Norway, France, Italy, Spain, and England, playwriting is still literature, with Chekhov and Ibsen and Shaw and Pirandello among the classics. American authors have on the whole worked less well for the stage than at storytelling, reporting, history, and polemics. Or to compare them with the novelists alone, no American playwright, not Tennessee Williams nor Thornton Wilder nor Edward Albee nor even Eugene O'Neill, has produced anything comparable in power to Herman Melville's *Moby Dick* or to the novels of Hawthorne, Henry James, Theodore Dreiser, John Dos Passos, and William Faulkner. It is *not* that Americans lack stage-sense. Our light musicals are today's world model, and we have produced both fiction films and documentaries of the highest prestige. Also our designs for dancing are original and often first-class. It is only on the speaking stage that show business has in America tended to be low business.

A good deal of this has been pointed out before; much of it is covered in a lecture I sometimes give called "America's Unrequited Love for Opera." Just now I am taking that love for granted, though you may not esteem it unrequited. And since so many of our composers are now writing operas, or planning to do so, I am going to take the liberty of suggesting certain things about the nature of opera which may be helpful.

Opera, let us understand this right off, is not light entertainment. It is drama at its most serious and most complete. It is also the most complex operation in music and the most complex in stage production. Even a circus is easier to mount.

Its complexity, moreover, involving the collaboration of poetry, visual design, and often dancing—along with music both vocal and instrumental—creates necessities that are more demanding than those of the concert. An opera is not a concert in costume. Neither is it just a play with music laid on. It is a dramatic action viewed through poetry and music, animated and controlled by its music, which is continuous. It owes to poetry much of its grandeur, to music all of its pacing. But since opera involves both intoned speech and mimed action, its pacing must permit both verbal clarity and convincing impersonation.

Now the opera is no such ancient form as verse tragedy, miracle plays, or even the light comedy with songs. It has a history of only four centuries and has never created a repertory in Spanish, Portuguese, Greek, Dutch, Polish, or the Scandinavian tongues, though it has enjoyed a certain popularity through translation in English and in Flemish. The twentieth century has witnessed sustained efforts, not yet wholly successful, toward making opera seem to grow naturally in the English and American languages. Whether these experiments can be stabilized remains undetermined, but the problems they raise are being labored at on both sides of the Atlantic.

For a successful outcome, certain preliminaries are essential. The composing fraternity must master the musical prosody of its language. This is in general better handled in the United Kingdom than in the United States. Over there the history of it all goes quite far back, to Henry VIII at least, and is preserved in libraries, remembered in the schools. Here the matter is neglected in schools and largely ignored in the homes where so many of our finest musical creators have grown up without ever hearing English spoken idiomatically.

For experimental opera productions, there needs to be available also a galaxy of young voices naturally well placed and with access to lessons. This situation is better on our side, Britain's colloquial speech, save for the Welsh and the Irish, being notably lacking in the nasal content necessary for differentiating vowels and for enabling them to cut through an orchestra. Canadian speech and South African are similarly soft, but Australian is very good for singing. That continent has long produced great voices; it may one day write operas for them.

In the matter of production Britain and the United States are both active, though they approach their opportunities differently. England lends its best facilities (Covent Garden, the English National Opera, and the big festivals) to its best composers. The works of Benjamin Britten, William Walton, Michael Tippett, and Peter Maxwell Davies have been effectively launched from these. Thea Musgrave, being a woman and Scottish, seems to get better treatment in America.

The opera houses of New York, Chicago, and San Francisco, on the other hand, though they have mounted works by composers as famous as Victor Herbert, Reginald De Koven, Deems Taylor, and Samuel Barber, seem not yet to have set a trend or created a school. Nor, for all its assiduities toward the contemporary, has Houston, Texas. Our most lively new operas have, with few exceptions, come out of the opera workshops in our colleges and universities. Among the exceptions are George Gershwin's *Porgy and Bess* and Marc Blitzstein's *Regina,* both of which originated in commercial theaters, and my own *Four Saints in Three Acts,* which began its playing life in an art museum, the Wadsworth Atheneum of Hartford, Connecticut. The University of Indiana, where John Eaton's *Cry of Clytemnestra* was first heard, has the finest facilities of any college for producing operas, also a remarkable voice faculty and nine theaters on campus. Columbia University's now-defunct Opera Workshop is deeply regretted. It is there that Menotti's *Medium* and my own *Mother Of Us All* were born. Unhappily, Columbia for a long time had no home for opera.* It once had, in the Brander Mathews Theatre, borrowed from the Drama Department, an ideal casting situation whereby professionals from the New York pool, all unpaid, could give time to students playing small roles and understudying large ones. Singing on a stage with even one artist of experience is like playing in an orchestra at the same desk with a professional. That sort of apprenticeship, though hard to come by, is unutterably valuable. And so, of

*On 15 September 1988 The Kathryn Bache Miller Theatre, at 116th Street and Broadway, was formally opened by Columbia University.

course, is hearing one's own composition conducted, staged, and sung by people who know what *cannot* be done in opera.

One of those things, believe me, is to "act," to simulate emotion by any means whatsoever except through the singing voice. Impersonation yes. That is created by costume and aided by a minimum of controlled movement (call it choreography if you like). But the emotions of high tragedy, insofar as these make up the substance of opera, are projected by the singing voice alone, not by any contributing circumstance. The popularity of opera recordings, which bear no visual aids to comprehension, has long been witness to this. Comic moments, let us admit, do permit a modicum of acting.

Regarding the advantages of British versus American production of operas in English, let us not underestimate the power of Great Britain's promotion machinery, which operates through its embassies and consulates. Henry Barraud, formerly music director of the French Radio and Television, told me not long after World War II that foreign pressures toward performance did not tend to come, as was commonly supposed, from the Soviet Union. "I don't hear twice a year from the Russians," he said, "but not a week goes by without my receiving a demand from the British Culture Office to perform some work by Benjamin Britten."

American artists' careers, on the contrary, practically all suffer from official neglect. The chief American composer to profit abroad from the State Department's blessing was George Gershwin, whose opera *Porgy and Bess* toured internationally, with partial government support, for two years. An opera of mine, *Four Saints in Three Acts,* got from the State Department a small contribution toward its Paris trip of 1952, and Douglas Moore's *Ballad of Baby Doe,* similarly blessed, went to Berlin and Yugoslavia. Otherwise, official encouragement for trips abroad has been generous to performing groups without specifying at all that U.S. music be played. And lecture tours have been awarded occasionally to composers. Unfortunately the countries where performance might help a composer professionally are likely to be omitted from the State Department's plan. England, France, Germany, Italy, and Scandinavia are not judged to be "sensitive areas" meriting the support that has regularly promoted good will toward our country in Turkey, Burma, India, the South American republics, and black Africa.

In any case, operas are being written all over the United States and the United Kingdom and many are produced, listened to, and internationally reviewed. Americans do tend, however, to go off half-cocked. They are without any serious mastery of the words-and-music techniques (and I mean orchestral accompaniment as well as word-setting). The British are limited in their productions by a lack of critical support from the universities and also by their music publishers, who, like most other British businesses, are monopoly-oriented. Literary publishers there, responsible to a longer and a grander history, still enjoy a somewhat competitive setup. English composers, however, unless they are pushed by the establishment, very frequently get squeezed out of distribution. The late Stanley Bate, a fecund and charming composer rarely heard today, is a case in point. Lord Berners is another.

Both countries have libretto trouble. The British tend to emulate their own literary classics—Sir Arthur Sullivan in *Ivanhoe,* Vaughan Williams in a version of Shakespeare's *Merry Wives of Windsor* called *Sir John in Love,* and in *Riders to the Sea* by John Millington Synge. Benjamin Britten, by using minor poets, major novelists, and slightly scabrous themes, was more successful. It is to foreign-language opera, however, not English, that Shakespeare, and once or twice Sir Walter Scott, have made their most valid contributions through (in Italian) *Lucia di Lammermoor, Hamlet, Falstaff, Macbeth,* and *Otello;* (in French) *Hamlet* and *Roméo et Juliette.* Let us not forget either how charmingly Britten has handled *A Midsummer Night's Dream.*

English masterpiece poetry in the original can throw almost any composer. The British suffer too from the lack of a solid history in composing for the stage, their musical strength lying mainly in the comic vein and the liturgical. Nor is there a history of serious libretto writing; both Nahum Tate's *Dido and Aeneas* and Dryden's multimedia *King Arthur,* though among the best, do skirt dangerously the tempting shallows of light verse. In general the British composer has neither found good serious librettos nor, with the exception of Britten's *Peter Grimes* (based on a poem of George Crabbe), shown marked ability for handling a dramatic theme.

The current American trend is to use for librettos cut-down versions of successful plays. The playwriting techniques of Eugène Scribe and Victorien Sardou applied to stories by Dumas *jeune,* Victor Hugo, and similar sources have produced in Europe such unshakable repertory works as *La Traviata, Rigoletto,* and *Tosca.* These same techniques applied to materials nondramatic in origin have caused the creation of *Faust* and *Carmen* and *Louise* (all faultless librettos). By pursuing this course of facile story-interest and by including lots of historical subject matter, libretto writing achieved in nineteenth-century France, Italy, and Germany an acceptable standard which replaced for a post-Revolutionary public the earlier models of Metastasio and da Ponte. Actually, libretto writing on the Continent has by now well over three centuries of history as a literary form that can be entrusted by those administering public funds to poets, or even to prose writers with a tolerance for music and some sense of the stage.

The American libretto, whether poetic or in prose, has suffered from the banality of American playwriting. Even music cannot bring to life its commonplace emotional occasions nor sustain its garrulous dialogue. I realize that dialogue is in general the American playwright's first gift, but even this at its compact best cannot hold up a tragedy of which the emotional content provokes no terror.

Invigorating the opera repertory by modernizing its musical textures and by introducing up-to-date story-themes are classical ways of keeping contemporary opera a part of the intellectual life. Any holding back in such matters by poets and composers is bound to discourage the endowed production agencies, which prefer a bold approach. Commercial producers—in films, television, or theater—are more timid. They like the excitements of novel sex, psychology, politics, mating manners, and religion; but they fear box-office failure for modern music.

Opera is rarely commercial; it is almost entirely endowed. Virtually none of it is self-supporting, not even the popular works of Richard Wagner and of Puccini. The whole operatic establishment, whether its funds be of capitalist origin, as with us, or Marxist-Leninist bureaucratic, as in Russia, is endowed, subsidized, tax-exempt. And its operators are subject to criticism for the way they spend public monies both by the press and by the head people of our universities, conservatories, and libraries, all of whom are also spending public monies. The results, for all the squabbling that goes on about "advanced" versus "conservative" repertory, is a higher degree of both freedom and responsibility in operatic production than is dreamed of in commercial show-biz.

There is actually lots of courage around, as well as money, for opera production. So much indeed that I wonder whether the timidities of opera composition in America and Britain may not be due more to underdeveloped musical skills than to hesitancies about subject matter. Certainly there is a dearth of strong librettos in the English-speaking countries.

Now let me go back to the beginnings of opera in the years just preceding

1600. We can do this because the basic format has since changed very little. The variations of this can be infinite, and the story-line is always a bit colored by local needs whenever the format moves into a new language. But that format must be preserved, or opera will fail to take root. In my view of it, the basic recipe reads somewhat as follows.

What, you may ask, is an opera anyway? It is a dramatic action involving impersonation, words, and music. Without impersonation it is a cantata. Without music, but with impersonation, it is a play. Without words, but with impersonation and music, it is a dance spectacle. With only impersonation it is a pantomime. Any of these can be comical, serious, or mixed.

A comic opera mainly impersonates without dignity, makes fun of us all, alternates jokes with musical numbers, lays charm on with a trowel.

A serious opera tells a mythological story which leads, unless interrupted by some superhuman agent, to a tragic outcome. The mixed comedy, or tragicomedy, is always, like Mozart's *Don Giovanni,* more tragic than comic.

Now what is a dramatic action? It is what happens inevitably to persons opposed to one another by character, circumstance, or desire. The energy leading to this outcome is latent in their differences of desire and in the unalterable nature of character.

It is not a drama unless events are described or mimed by actors impersonating the characters involved.

It is not an opera unless both words and action are expressed through music and carried forward by it.

It is not a satisfactory opera unless the words, the action, and the circumstance are made more vivid through music than they could ever be without. Because words sung carry farther than words spoken (or even shouted); because instrumental music can intensify suspense or calm, explosions of energy or its complete arrest; and because landscapes, weather, history and its monuments, all sorts of contributory detail can be evoked by musical device.

This is not to say that musical tragedy is grander than poetic tragedy. The fact is simply that after opera came into existence in any language, poetic tragedy became a thing of the past, however glorious, with opera taking over the contemporary effort toward complete theater.

Moreover, your spectacle will not hold the stage, unless the story of it, the dramatic action, moves forward. Otherwise you may be left with a static spectacle on your hands—something like an oratorio in costume, Stations of the Cross, or a song-cycle.

Music, please remember, is the great animator. Without it dancing goes dead and so do liturgies. Only spoken plays can survive without it. Even films and television spectacles tend to freeze up, just as dancing does, without musical help. Music is warming, emotional, acoustically surrounding, a bath. The visual always keeps a certain distance, hence is cooler than the musical experience. Lincoln Kirstein says, "The life of a ballet is the life of its musical score," meaning that when the dancers are no longer moved (literally) by the music, the work drops out of repertory.

Let's look at this musical element, the slippery substance that can so firmly change the specific gravity of anything. Seriously employed, it is a "noble" material, and for any serious subject needs to be carefully composed and carefully executed. The slapdash may go down in nightclubs or drinking joints. Similarly for casually selected materials and for their arrangement in some accidentally determined order. Such elements are too frail to sustain a serious mythological subject or to prepare us for a tragic ending.

While we are discussing mythology, let us stipulate that history, fairy tales, lives of the saints, anything anybody can almost believe can be subsumed under that head. From *Samson et Dalila* through *Cenerentola*, *Tannhäuser*, and *Boris Godunov* to *Madama Butterfly*, *Giovanna d'Arco*, and *Billy the Kid*, all are believable stories about believable people. And music makes these people seem bigger, blows them up to mythological size. It even overblows them toward collapse in the case of Cinderella (who is hence better for dancing than for song). Also for the super-monumental and political (say George Washington, Napoleon, Abraham Lincoln). Singing could only diminish them.

But let us say you have a sizable heroine or hero in mind. How do you go about procuring a libretto? My own way is to address myself to a poet. This is dangerous because English-language poets have over the last century and a half been most of them quite clumsy at handling a dramatic action. They can't avoid talking in their own person, seem unable to write dialogue objectively. But I think there is no way around that. The poets must simply re-educate themselves if they are at all stagestruck.

How they can do this I do not know. But I am sure that the poets who have no innate stage-instinct (that well-known *sens du théâtre*) cannot be taught it, though a latent stage-sense can perhaps be brought to life. The matter is a difficult one. If the composer himself has a feeling for the stage, that fact solves only half the problem. But it may help him in choosing a poet. If he does not have it he should leave opera alone, and if he cannot pick a poet who also has a bit of it, their collaboration is not likely to produce a viable stage work. There is no final test of that, of course, short of full-scale production. The history of every opera establishment is strewn with costly failures.

It is just possible that further research into the history of libretto writing may reveal standards by which the English-language libretto can be adjudged a legitimate poetic form. If so, then the poets may come to face it without thinking of themselves as betraying their art. Actually poets are less fearful of music (they all love being set) than of the stage itself.

Opera, to be worth looking up to, has to be poetic theater. And librettos, I think, are best when custom-built. Readymades, even in the form of a well-structured prose play cut down to libretto size, are rarely satisfactory in English. They are not even literature, chopped up like that, pinched here and let out there to accommodate musico-emotional timings, which are quite different from the verbo-emotional.

By musical versus verbal timings I do not mean that communicating emotion to an audience by words alone takes any more time, or less, than by music or by words and music. On the contrary, a strong emotion can be extended in any medium to last, say, twenty minutes, if sufficient variety of texture is available. But twenty minutes of speech will pour out more words than twenty minutes of music can handle. A love scene from *Romeo and Juliet* set to music as recitative would be jabber; and if set uncut as cantilena, with all the vocal extensions needed to make singing eloquent, could seem interminable. Too many words can get in music's way. So also, I may add, can too many notes obscure the text.

A libretto needs to be, in general, much shorter than a play. Otherwise it may lack flexibility for being fitted into musical continuities. It also needs poetic language. Not pompous language, nor florid, nor overloaded with imagery. But nobly plain, if possible compact, and somehow appropriate to myth-size characters.

An opera libretto must be animated by its music, and the emotional progress of the drama must conform to musico-emotional timings, not speech-play timings. To sustain and extend to its acceptable limit any musico-emotional situation, the use of structural devices specific to music is the available method, the only method. This is what is meant by the earliest Italian name for opera, *dramma per musica,* as well as by Richard Wagner's demand that his own theater works be referred to as *Musikdrama.*

For the best musical result, poetic textures and all characterizations need to be a little plainer than for spoken tragedy, and an excess of visual imagery is to be avoided.

In my opinion, plots, intrigues, and planned suspense, however exciting they may be on the comic stage or in melodrama, tend to make a tragic outcome seem not inevitable. Operas based on legend, myth, fairy tale, biography, or national history tend therefore to be both poetically and musically richer than those corseted by a tight play-structure.

Complex musico-dramatic structures dealing with humor and sentiment or with satire are not an uncommon variant of "serious" opera. Mozart's *Marriage of Figaro* and its companion-piece Rossini's *Barber of Seville,* Wagner's *Meistersinger von Nürnberg,* Strauss's *Rosenkavalier,* Verdi's *Falstaff,* and Puccini's *Gianni Schicchi* are notorious cases in which the domination of a whole work by its musical continuity has turned comedy into a serious enterprise. Actually these works, which survive almost exclusively in the larger houses, are far more monumental than funny.

The comic speaking-stage shows no history of growth, development, or decline since the earliest antiquity, in the West since Greece and Rome. The tragic stage in poetry, on the other hand, has a history. It matures in any language once, then dies, leaving behind monuments of literature that live forever.

The tragic opera, a late invention, has not yet died out in any language. It has left us moreover three legacies previously unknown—the proscenium stage, the pit orchestra (a curtain of instrumental sound through which all is filtered), and the monumental singing voice.

The comic musical stage, liturgical ceremonies, and song recitals do not, in general, require great vocal range or power. The tragic musical stage, the opera, or *dramma per musica,* had perfected by the middle 1630s a training for loudness and flexibility in all the vocal ranges (as well as a name for it, *bel canto*) that has survived to this day as the training system for operatic voices, those with a minimum range of two octaves at all levels of loudness. Operas are still written to be sung by such voices, and pit orchestras in our opera houses are also of monumental proportions, rarely fewer than fifty players.

Such is the equipment available today in the professional houses, the conservatories, and the colleges. It also includes usually some kind of built or painted scenery, artificial lighting, appropriate costuming, and a modicum of controlled stage-action.

I say a modicum because with any musical production being completely rehearsed and always conducted, and with today's other popular serious stage medium, the dance, equally controlled and regulated, it is not wise to allow singers to improvise their "acting." Still less is it wise to allow stage directors the kind of freedom toward distortions and even contradictions of the stated dramatic action that have lately been current.

On the other hand, singers are neither dancers nor acrobats. Excessive pantomime is not suitable to vocalists or to their bodies, which need to save breath for singing. The best solution of the "acting" problem is to use choreographers with a sense of music and some taste, for moving the singers around (with grace if possible, and minimally) so that at major musical moments they can stand still in a good acoustical spot and proceed to act with the voice, which is after all what the art of singing is.

Enabling singers to make words clear and meaningful is part of the composer's art. Another is to reveal character and feelings by musical device. This may be operated within the vocal line, as with Mozart and the Italians, or by orchestral means, as with Wagner and many French composers.* In any case, specific expressivity is more easily achieved through line, vocal or instrumental, than through harmony, the latter being highly valuable for structure, for holding our attention on the expressive line. Orchestration too may be useful in pointing things up. Extreme variety in the orchestra, however, though delicious in concert music, can seem finicky in opera, as it so often does with Berlioz and Rimsky-Korsakov. Wagner, Debussy, Mozart, Verdi, even Stravinsky, have offered more dependable support to the expressive element by keeping orchestral color steady and clearly related at all times to the voice. Never forget that no matter how interesting orchestral sound may seem, singing is what opera is about. And this is as true of Wagner's stage works as of Bellini's. Actually Wagner's music-dramas are today opera's chief vehicles for power vocalism. In every house they receive the most careful musical treatment and offer us the grandest voices.

So let us restate the situation in reverse order.

Opera is singing. This singing is both monumental and flexible—loud, soft, high, low, fast, slow.

---

*An example of characterization by vocal line is the coloratura of the flighty young page Oscar in Verdi's *Ballo in maschera*. On the other hand, it is orchestral chord-sequences that identify with such massive weight Wotan's Valhalla in Wagner's "Ring," and with evasiveness Debussy's Mélisande.

THE NATURE OF OPERA

Wagner, Das Rheingold, *scene 2*

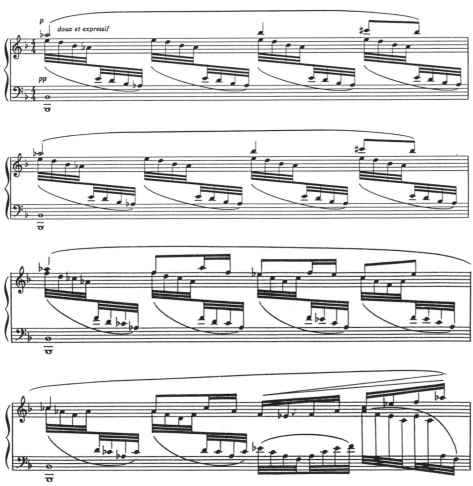

Debussy, Pelléas et Mélisande

Opera exposes through impersonation and poetic dialogue a serious dramatic action. This is a serious action because it faces at all times the possibility of a tragic outcome. And it is moved forward toward whatever outcome may be its destiny by instrumental music and by singing. A dramatic action is opera's thread and purpose. Poetry is its explanatory method. Singing is its sine qua non, its language.

As regards the words-and-music factor, that is a constant in any mature language, established early on by composers, and is not likely to alter much after that. So that the vocal line of Italian music, or French or English or German or Russian, tends to remain closely tied to the classical pronunciation of those languages.

Other musical textures, however, such as harmonic and contrapuntal styles, rhythmic devices and orchestral coloration, insofar as these are expressed instrumentally, vary with history and fashion. From Monteverdi to Nono, from Rameau to Poulenc, from Purcell to Britten, from Schütz to Schönberg, and Glinka to Stravinsky, the voice-parts of operas and oratorios in any language are almost interchangeable, though their instrumental accompaniments can vary from Baroque, Rococo, and Romantic to polytonal, nontonal, even twelve-tone serial. Excellent opera music has indeed been composed in all these manners.

A similar history seems to obtain for librettos. Opera stories certainly have varied far less in the last four centuries than has good poetic diction. Dryden, Molière, Metastasio, Racine, Goethe, Maeterlinck, von Hofmannsthal, Claudel, T. S. Eliot, W. H. Auden, and Gertrude Stein have all, in consequence, served effectively the lyric stage.

My recipe for the structure of serious opera, as stated above, is the classical one and not likely to be radically altered. In the domain of stylistic orientation, however, poetic as well as musical, anything goes, provided the voice parts are correctly prosodized, and can be heard clearly through the other kinds of sound.

Now let us suppose you have an opera, well written for the words and for the voices that are to sing them, embodying a story line, or myth, that the authors consider worthy and touching, the whole supported throughout by appropriate instrumental music. Let us suppose also that you have an offer of production under reputable circumstances. How do you go about protecting your conception?

If you cannot procure for the occasion a producing director whom you trust to understand your dramatic concept, you are out of luck. Stage directors, designers, costumers, and choreographers, all working along different stylistic lines (and with no deep knowledge of the script, plus none at all of the music), will turn your work into a variety show. Musical direction and casting are less of a hazard, since the conductor will surely have read the score. But miming and movements, as improvised by the stage director, and the clumsy efforts of singers to act while singing, will be very hard to correct unless your producer is friendly.

Singers, let me say it firmly, must not be allowed to stagger, lurch, weave about, or make faces. Musical expression comes from singing the words and the music, not from mugging. Nor from doing anything else while singing. Any movement required should be done at other times, between phrases, never on the phrase, except in comedy.

Neither should singing ever be done in profile. Maximum beauty of sound and maximum verbal clarity come from facing the audience. With a quarter-turn, half the sound and sense are lost. With a half-turn, you lose three-fourths of the words. Singing at full turn, back to the audience, can be used occasionally for dramatic effect, but only on clear vowels sung *ff.* No consonants will carry. Conversations in opera can be very effective with all faces turned out, hands and arms being used to identify the person addressed. To look at people when they sing, that offers them attention. Let them also look at you when you sing. But everybody, while singing, must look straight out, even in love-duets. There is no other way to assure a musical balance or to hear the words.

The acoustical necessities of opera, different from those of the spoken stage, require therefore, instead of the improvised bits of "business" that so often light up spoken dialogue, a form of regulated movement not far from what the dance world calls choreography. In opera the music is completely planned; in ballet so is the dancing. In serious opera all stage movements should be agreed upon and directed. When this is done, the singing improves, characterization clears up, and emotion communicates.

The planning of such movement, with all attention to acoustical needs and to full visibility between singers and conductor, can be done quite early in the rehearsal time. A *Sitzprobe,* or seated rehearsal, though valuable for musical cueing and for choral balances, need not involve intense expression. (Some singers will always be "saving their voices" anyway.) It is in the later rehearsals and the early run-throughs, after movements and positions have been set, that individual expression and an interplay of feeling can be encouraged. These will for the most part come about automatically, once they have been facilitated by appropriate gestures and positions. In my recommendations for operatic staging, expressive intensity is never demanded until the moves and positions are right. Then it comes without asking and can be further refined in coaching sessions with the répétiteur.

Moves and positions are a matter of stylistic authenticity, hence of choreographic taste. Every opera needs a stage-director aware of acoustical needs and of singers' limitations, but for the best musical results he needs a co-director skilled in dance expression and in regional ways. English characters, for example, do not move like Italians. Neither do French or Germans.

Regarding the cuts that many conductors make, all I can suggest is that they be tried out in rehearsal. Then, if both the composer and the librettist are consenting (but only then) leave them in during the early performances. After all, nothing, during the first years of an opera's life, is to be thought of as permanent. This remark applies strongly to interventions of the stage-director. With the conductor matters are different; by the fifth performance all tempos and volume levels should be firm, the pacings too, even the overall timing of the show. And his markings can then pretty safely be considered as part of the score.

As a last word, let me preach a little to the poets. It is a good two hundred years now since a sense of the stage was expected of you. Some, nevertheless, have still a certain yearning for the boards, and all of you, I think, like to hear your lovely verses sung. The opera libretto may be a secondary form, but it is a worthy one, honored by many of poetry's best names, just as incidental music to poetic plays has been composed by practically all of music's great ones. And don't be afraid of asking help from someone instinctively wise in stage matters. W. H. Auden, by himself theatrically weak, with the help of Chester Kallman made his work stick on the stage, even the singing stage, the most demanding of them all.

And don't get mixed up with composers who have no respect for poetry, who think they can pick up a plot just anywhere and treat their librettist like a hired man. The subject of serious opera has to be something that touches both you and the composer deeply enough to inspire you both through long labor. Opera writing, in my view, is a two-man job. It takes a poet and a composer, working at the same theme, to pull it off. It also helps if they can bear each other's company for the length of time they may be working together. But if they share a liking for the opera's theme, that should be fairly easy. That and keeping other poets' and other composers' noses out of the enterprise.

CHAPTER TWELVE

After All

Now let us sum up.

How to write music for English words is the problem. It cannot be solved by imposing a procedure. Every work is different, and so is each composer's mind. Nevertheless, there are choices to make, and whether these are better made step by step or in unplanned jumps is moot. For now I shall merely enumerate things to be done.

1. A text in prose or in verse, whether chosen or imposed, must be there for working on; and the composer must have accepted it. Some texts will turn out to be hopeless for music, others unsuitable for present use. Instinct and experience must be the guide.

2. Laying the text out in word-groups will at some point help toward clarifying both the plain meaning (if there is one) and its expression, its rhetoric.

3. Selecting a vocal range to suit the text and the occasion will save time. Many concert songs can later be transposed, of course, quite satisfactorily. Arias have too wide a range to allow much shifting.

4. By now you will be looking for what I call a "musical idea," a way of turning the text into a tune. This may or may not involve vertical intervallic relations, a harmony, whether expressed in full or merely present by moments. In either case you can now start composing a vocal line. This, if it fits the words for both sound and sentiment, will be itself your "musical idea," which subsequent additions and corrections will merely amplify. And let us remember that developments can proceed as effectively by contrast as by similarities.

5. An instrumental accompaniment, at its simplest, should:
   (a) help the listeners to follow the tune
   (b) help the singers to carry the tune; keep them on pitch
   (c) not obscure the verbal text by attracting undue attention.

6. It can also do these things in a more sophisticated manner, reinforcing

expression at the same time by illustrating the text. Illustration can be either visual (linear), visceral (kinetic), or emotional (with spinal chills).

7. It can situate a scene:

    (a) by geographic, ethnographic, or sociological references

    (b) by evoking historic musical styles

    (c) by depicting weather, animated or calm

    (d) by suggesting water, foliage in motion, clouds, crowds, animals, or birds.

8. It can set off a florid vocal line by contrasted monotonies of:

    (a) rhythm, in an identical meter or in a quite different one

    (b) abstractions such as the "Alberti bass" (oom-pah), scales, arpeggios, even chords not clearly related to the vocal line but rhythmically distributed.

9. If there is to be no tonal accompaniment at all, then the singer or singers must be able to stay on pitch without it, which is rare. There are, of course, clandestine ways of helping them out, such as concealing woodwinds among the choral singers, or a small pianoforte behind them. And the prompter, from his box, can usually, by singing along, lead wandering soloists back to the pitch.

10. In all cases, especially those in which the accompaniment itself is part of the "musical idea," the instrumental contribution must take the lead, give tempos and pacings, create a musical structure and sustain it. Only a skilled accompanist or an experienced orchestral conductor can do this. No vocalist can handle with freedom a vocal line or a dramatic one without a sustained music line for support.

11. When any song, or longer work, seems finished, read it through quickly for wrong notes, many of which will correct themselves in rehearsal anyway.

12. Read it through again, this time for continuity, line, trajectory. If at any point it fails to hold your attention, it is sure to lose interest right there for listeners. Correct these points carefully, maybe cutting, which is always easier to do than to add or to rework.

A long-line trajectory is as important for short works as it is for long ones and for sections of long ones. To achieve this, some quite ruthless cutting may be necessary; you will not regret it. You can restore the cuts later if you find a better solution.

Also, I suggest aiming for continuity in all the contributing elements. I mean by this that the vocal line itself should make a composition. The accompaniment too, even when it is as simple as an oom-pah, and harmony must also make a pattern, a chorale, as the French call it. So too the sequence of orchestral colorations. Every element of the work needs to have a way of beginning, of going on, and of ending. Pay attention to matters like these, and you will be paid back in rapt attention from your listeners. Also in the freedom and ease of expression you will be providing to your interpreters.

13. Do not attempt to have an opinion about your work, to review it, so to speak. If you like to write for some imaginary audience, then that audience must consist only of yourself and strangers.

14. Your collaborators on any enterprise are always, of course, to be taken seriously. They are your team. Musicians working together, hearing together, feeling together, and projecting together, that is the miracle, the experience we prize above all others. And its parallel delight, which is working together with respected colleagues in a theater, or on a film set, can be no less rewarding when through a similar miracle you turn out, all of you, to be "working on the same show," rather than on five highly different versions of it. This kind of thing does not happen every day, but when it does it gets remembered on both sides of the curtain.

Musical Illustrations from the
Works of Virgil Thomson

MUSICAL ILLUSTRATIONS

"La Valse grégorienne"

Four poems depict the waking dreams of a very young man. These include memories of childhood, also of an amorous adventure. "Dahlias of the mist," I suggest, refers to streetlights (of Paris no doubt) seen through a heavy fog.

The main musical idea of the work is an oom-pah accompaniment in waltz time, to keep the melody moving along, later to itemize syllables by adding four counts to the still continuing three. The three are alone and steady for the waking up; then there is in-time chanting to intensify recall of the adventure.

Making a sustained musical composition out of four poems was the problem. The simplest of abstractions—oom-pah rhythm and chordally accompanied chant— were the unifying agents.

One note per syllable, counting as such all mute vowels, is standard procedure in setting French poetry. So is the occasional omission of a final mute in lines that evoke either childhood or the colloquial.

The vocal range of an eleventh, D–G for soprano, avoids any need for strain. The mood is poetic, not declamatory.

MUSICAL ILLUSTRATIONS

II. Grenadine
Pomegranate

l'eau se couv-rait de bles-su-res. Gre-
wa-ters were cov-ered with scars. Pome-

na-de grena-di-ne, grenad' ou-vert' sur un ta-pis. Ah!
gra-nate gre-na-dine,___ pome-gra-nate clo-ven on a cloth. A-

pen-dant que l'on dî-ne comm' les en-fants s'en-nui-ent. Faut-il que l'on nous
las, at din-ner time how___ bored the chil-dren are! Why must they tell us

di-se des bê-ti-ses à l'in-ter-nat: vous pre-nez pour u-
such id-i-o-tic things in board-ing school? You may think that's a

ne va-li-se ce fruit au ja-bot gre-nat. S'il é-tait un' va-
suit-case, not a fruit that wears a gar-net tie. And if it were a

"LA VALSE GRÉGORIENNE"

li - se, qu'y ran-ge - ri - ez vous? Les é - toi-les qu'on di - vi - ni - se
suit - case what would you put in - side? The stars that you myth - o - lo - gize

où les se - crets de vos coeurs fous?
or the se - crets of your fool hearts?

III. La Rosée
Dew

Tant d'oi - seaux, ce ma - tin, sont en -
So ma - ny birds this morn - ing have

trés dans ma cham - bre que je cher - che le jour
en - tered my room that how - ev - er I try seek -

sans par - ve - nir à me ré - veil - ler. Tant de rou - geurs, ce ma -
- ing the day - light I can - not wake. So ma - ny reds in the

IV. Le Wagon Immobile - *The Motionless Box-car*

"LA VALSE GRÉGORIENNE"

bri - tais ma fray - eur au-près des lé - preux,
shel - tered my ter - ror a - mong the le - pers,

j'y ai vu la mai - son où j'a - bri -
there I saw a - gain the house___ where once I

tais mon a - mour. Fil - le per - du - e dans les ru -
shel - tered___ my love. Girl gone a - stray in the al - ley -

el - les et par - mi les dah - lias des brouil-lards,
ways and a - mong the dah - lias of the mist,

a - vons nous des souv'-
are there mem - o - ries

nirs com - muns? A - vez vous pleu - ré, ce
we can share? Have you shed tears, as I

MUSICAL ILLUSTRATIONS

Published by Southern Music Publishing Co., New York.

Copyright © 1940 and 1967 by Virgil Thomson.

MUSICAL ILLUSTRATIONS

"Susie Asado"

The text is said to portray a Spanish dancer, though certainly birds are present. In any case the composer's music-idea in both voice and piano is an evocation of bird sounds.

The accompaniment consists of musical abstractions only—broken triads, rising scales (in sevenths), open fifths stacked up (C, G, D), and a single tone with an appoggiatura added to make it twitter.

LYRICS: Gertrude Stein

MUSICAL ILLUSTRATIONS

"SUSIE ASADO"

ren-der clean must. Drink pups. Drink pups drink pups lease a sash hold

see it shine_ and a bo - bo - link has_ pins. It shows a nail.

What is a nail._ A nail is un-is-on. Sweet, sweet, sweet, sweet, sweet tea._

"English Usage"

A free recitative punctuated by short major chords.

LYRICS:
Marianne Moore

MUSICAL ILLUSTRATIONS

"Before Sleeping"

An evocation of childhood, not an imitation of it. Counting the melodic voice as one part, the whole consists of two- and three-part counterpoint, including a few measures in which two of the accompanying voices are in chords.

These verses can be sung in almost "white voice," the "Amen" completely white, which is to say, without vibrato.

MUSICAL ILLUSTRATIONS

"BEFORE SLEEPING"

Je-sus Christ de-liv-er me. He's the branch and I'm the flow'r. Pray God send me a hap-py hour. And if I die be-fore I wake, I pray that Christ my soul will take. A - men.

From *Praises and Prayers*.
Published by G. Schirmer, Inc., New York.

MUSICAL ILLUSTRATIONS

"Take, O, Take Those Lips Away"

The melody is arpeggiated, the accompaniment guitarlike. It also suggests the horn.

According to Shakespeare, the events take place in Vienna, a locale long associated musically with the sound of hunting-horns.

LYRICS: Shakespeare's *Measure for Measure*

"TAKE, O, TAKE THOSE LIPS AWAY"

Published by Southern Music Publishing Co., New York.

MUSICAL ILLUSTRATIONS

"Sigh No More, Ladies"

The song and its accompaniment recall the fandango, also the Spanish guitar, vastly popular during Elizabethan times. There is no overt attempt to take us to Venice, though Spain, as the chief world power, was felt as strongly there as in England.

The hey-nonny refrain is patter, probably of English origin.

Like "Take, O, Take," this song is for a man.

LYRICS: Shakespeare's *Merchant of Venice*

★ Pronounced "heevy"

"SIGH NO MORE, LADIES"

MUSICAL ILLUSTRATIONS

"The Feast of Love"

The rhythm is a simultaneous six-against-four, the instrumentation percussive. The music throughout celebrates all-night dancing and song in praise of Venus, exactly as described in the Latin poem.

LYRICS: *Pervigilium Veneris*, anonymous Latin, second or fourth century; translated by Virgil Thomson

"THE FEAST OF LOVE"

know-ing. She who loves___ cou-pling lov-ers has made the myr-tle tents___

And un-der bird-fill'd___ trees___ leads dance with song;___ To-mor-row all shall

love; Ve-nus com-mands. ___ All shall___ love___ to-mor-row, All___ who___ have___ nev - er loved.

Published by G. Schirmer, Inc., New York.

MUSICAL ILLUSTRATIONS

"Tiger! Tiger!"

The original is for baritone and orchestra.

Its middle section depicts a lamb, then returns to the tiger in his jungle.

LYRICS: William Blake

"TIGER! TIGER!"

From *Five Songs from William Blake*.
Published by Southern Music Publishing Co., New York.

MUSICAL ILLUSTRATIONS

"The Tiger"

This earlier setting of the same poem for soprano voice with piano has a non-expressive middle section, designed to throw into relief the sixty-four-thousand-dollar question about God, who must have created both innocence and evil.

The last part of this version returns to its opening, with a factorylike rhythm of five counts running consecutively against the four-four of the proclamation.

LYRICS: William Blake

"THE TIGER"

bright In the for - ests of the night,

What im-mor - tal hand or eye Dare

frame_ thy_ fear - ful_ sym-me-try.

MUSICAL ILLUSTRATIONS

"The Land of Dreams"

This is a miniature drama between a child and his widowed father.

It awakens the boy as with a trumpet, then describes with double-chord harmonies the landscape of his dream, where he thinks he saw his mother "among the lambs" (briefly evoked), "clothed in white" and walking with is father "in sweet delight."

The father then recounts (on the cello) his own efforts toward the visionary. The six-tone harmonies here are less ethereal.

The boy's reply, again in double harmonies, opts for his dreamworld as "better far" than anything experienced awake.

In his book with Kathleen O'Donnell Hoover, *Virgil Thomson: His Life and Music,* John Cage finds all this musical depiction a bit excessive. That, of course, is a matter of taste. In any case the two characters speak differently, and their emotions are different. This makes the poem a little drama, a two-character play.

LYRICS: William Blake

"THE LAND OF DREAMS"

MUSICAL ILLUSTRATIONS

"THE LAND OF DREAMS"

From *Five Songs from William Blake.*
Published by Southern Music Publishing Co., New York.
Copyright © 1953 and 1981 by Virgil Thomson.

MUSICAL ILLUSTRATIONS

"Rose-cheeked Laura, Come"

The original version of these songs is for a mezzo-soprano of operatic range, the accompaniment for clarinet, viola, and harp. They are also published for mixed choir (SATB), arranged by the composer, as well as in this version for voice and piano.

The excerpt illustrates a flowing voice-line interwoven with the instrumental ones to produce, it is hoped, a musical texture matching the richness of the verses.

The blending of a mezzo-soprano voice with viola and clarinet can in fact be pretty sumptuous, with harmonies picked out by the brightness of the harp.

LYRICS: Thomas Campion

"ROSE-CHEEKED LAURA, COME"

From *Four Songs to Poems of Thomas Campion*.

Published by Southern Music Publishing Co., New York.

Copyright © 1953 and 1981 by Virgil Thomson.

MUSICAL ILLUSTRATIONS

Four Saints in Three Acts

The prologue to *Four Saints in Three Acts* exposes the chief musical materials of the opera.

These are, in addition to melodies derived naturalistically from the text, oom-pah chords in three-four time, triads of the tonic and dominant, churchlike chant, and the usual recitative. There is choral writing both in the madrigal manner and in hymn style. Harmonies are as plain as possible, always of service to the singing.

The orchestra is dominated in the fuller passages by an accordion, valuable for its organlike sostenuto, its richness in chords, and its extraordinary power of accent.

The opening idea is a wide-swung tune in four-four accompanied by an oom-pah in waltz time, quarter notes in the two meters remaining equal.

LIBRETTO: Gertrude Stein

Avila. *Steps and portal of the cathedral, the latter closed off by a small curtain (Curtain II).*

FOUR SAINTS IN THREE ACTS

Chor. I: saints pre-pare for saints it makes it well well fish it makes it well fish pre-pare for saints.

MUSICAL ILLUSTRATIONS

Four Saints in Three Acts, act 1

Act I begins with solo chanting, verbal flexibilities being contrasted with the plainest of organlike chords, all in strict tempo. This rigidity is followed by nonmeasured chanting and consistently interrupted by chorus II (small and mobile) and by chorus I (larger and stationary).

The antiphonal effect is ceremonial. The whole opera, in fact, can be conceived as a ritual. Actually the work when first completed, dominated as it is by choirs and by chanting, was less like an opera than an oratorio *about* an opera. It was not until Maurice Grosser, with his sympathy for both text and music (Stein used to say, "Maurice understands my writing"), had devised a plan for staging the work, a scenario, a choreography for moving singers about, that it became recognizable clearly as opera. It is still given in concert style, like a *Sitzprobe,* but in its definitive and final form it is unquestionably a stage work.

Tableau I   A garden at Avila in early Spring.   There is a wall and a tree.   St. Teresa II is seated under the tree painting flowers on very large eggs.

Published by G. Schirmer, Inc., New York.

Copyright © 1933 and 1960 by Virgil Thomson.

MUSICAL ILLUSTRATIONS

Four Saints in Three Acts, act 1

This ecstatic recitative for baritone consists of a descending scale, repeated seven times, with rhythms varied according to the text. The accompaniment is a chime rendered deeper by double bass and bassoon, which act as resonators.

Published by G. Schirmer, Inc., New York.

Copyright © 1933 and 1960 by Virgil Thomson.

MUSICAL ILLUSTRATIONS

Four Saints in Three Acts, act 1

This carol for soprano and flute is accompanied by pizzicato string chords, which observe a repeating pattern of their own rather than always supporting the voice-line.

FOUR SAINTS IN THREE ACTS

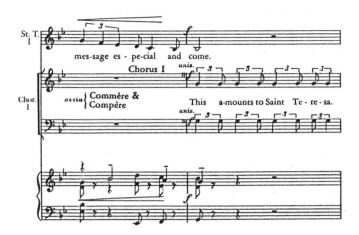

Published by G. Schirmer, Inc., New York.

MUSICAL ILLUSTRATIONS

Four Saints in Three Acts, finale of act 2

A pantomime, or *scena,* for orchestra alone is explained in a tenor solo answered by soprano and mezzo-soprano. The tenor's final word takes place on a high A, pianissimo.

FOUR SAINTS IN THREE ACTS

MUSICAL ILLUSTRATIONS

The Mother of Us All

This hymnlike music opens a wedding scene. The melody it accompanies is both declamatory and arpeggiated. The hymn-style accompaniment suggests also horns and trumpets. A blending of string sounds with brasses is used frequently in this opera to characterize the leading soprano.

LIBRETTO: Gertrude Stein

THE MOTHER OF US ALL

(*Jo the Loiterer leads in Indiana Elliot in wedding attire, followed by John Adams and Constance Fletcher, and followed by Daniel Webster and Angel More. All the other characters follow after. Anne and Jenny Reefer come and stand by Susan B. Ulysses S. Grant sits down in a chair right behind the procession.*)

Published by G. Schirmer, Inc., New York

Copyright © 1947 and 1975 by Virgil Thomson.

MUSICAL ILLUSTRATIONS

The Mother of Us All

The finale of this work is a solo for the leading soprano, now become a statue of herself "in marble and gold."

Its music recalls the wedding hymn and includes as new material a funeral hymn.

The subdominant cadence at the end is suggestive of a Protestant "Amen."

THE MOTHER OF US ALL

THE MOTHER OF US ALL

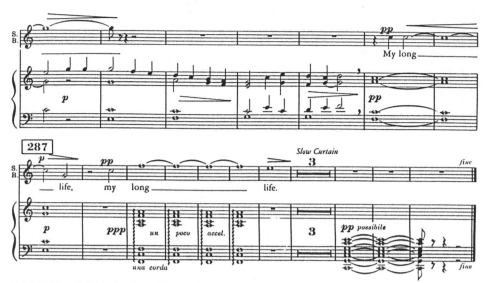

MUSICAL ILLUSTRATIONS

Lord Byron

Lord Byron is here "getting close," as one says, to the lady whom he eventually will marry.

The voice-line is tenorlike and showy, perhaps a shade insincere.

Eighth-notes in the orchestra keep it moving along. Otherwise the accompaniment is designed throughout to lend the singer a certain warmth.

LIBRETTO: Jack Larson

LORD BYRON

Published by Southern Music Publishing Co., New York.

MUSICAL ILLUSTRATIONS

Lord Byron

Lord Byron and Augusta Leigh, his half-sister, sing this love-duet.
The poem is Byron's own, with a change from "she" to "you."
The accompaniment is richly supportive of the voices.
There is no hint of insincerity.

LORD BYRON

MUSICAL ILLUSTRATIONS

Lord Byron

This trio for Byron, his wife, and his half-sister is playful music, including the accompaniment, though it is also, wherever support seems needed, of help to the singers.

LORD BYRON

MUSICAL ILLUSTRATIONS

LORD BYRON

MUSICAL ILLUSTRATIONS

LORD BYRON

Published by Southern Music Publishing Co., New York.

MUSICAL ILLUSTRATIONS

Lord Byron

A trio with words by Byron and music in the madrigal style.
    Though the accompaniment is minimal, the harmony is always clear.

LORD BYRON

MUSICAL ILLUSTRATIONS

Lord Byron

A trio, two of the voices off-stage.

The descending scales give motion to the scene, which is in itself static, helping it to move toward an ending after the situation has been fully exposed.

This scene shows plainly the isolaton of Byron's half-sister, pregnant at the time of his marriage.

There is no dramatic movement here, nor any development of the story line, only a musical structure. This moves toward a purely musical ending, after allowing sufficient time for its contrasted emotions to be shared with the audience.

LORD BYRON

MUSICAL ILLUSTRATIONS

LORD BYRON

MUSICAL ILLUSTRATIONS

LORD BYRON

MUSICAL ILLUSTRATIONS

Death of General Washington
arranged for mixed chorus (SATB) and keyboard

This is one of four "white spirituals" published under the group title *Southern Hymns*.

In music of this type neither open nor consecutive fifths were avoided.

The example is of an American musical species known to historians as hymn-and-fuguing-tune.

DEATH OF GENERAL WASHINGTON

MUSICAL ILLUSTRATIONS

DEATH OF GENERAL WASHINGTON

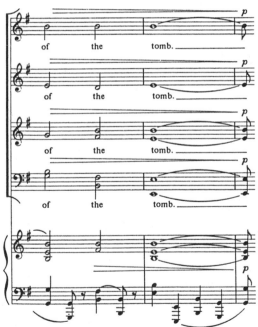

From *Southern Hymns*.
Published by Southern Music Publishing Co., New York.

MUSICAL ILLUSTRATIONS

Crossing Brooklyn Ferry
for mixed voices (SATB) and piano

The poem is by Walt Whitman.

The piano part aims chiefly to establish the just-barely-rocking motion of the ferryboat.

The text describes a diversified urban crowd.

The classical masters have never hesitated to presume that members of a vocal ensemble need not always be singing the same words at the same time. Confusion can be avoided by repeating ideas and phrases, also by remembering that many texts, especially the liturgical, are quite familiar anyway.

Singing about crowds while keeping the poet's diction uncrowded was the source of some effort. To manipulate choral masses so that they seem to be moving independently, that is ever the aim in staging crowd scenes; and such was the hope here in passages where the contrapuntal elements are not homogeneous.

CROSSING BROOKLYN FERRY

CROSSING BROOKLYN FERRY

MUSICAL ILLUSTRATIONS

MUSICAL ILLUSTRATIONS

Missa pro defunctis, Introit

for men's choir (TTBB), women's choir (SSAA),
and orchestra (3333, 4331, hp., timp., perc., str.)

The Latin text of the Mass for the Dead is no longer used in Roman Catholic churches. This is therefore, like many another Mass in large format, strictly a concert work.

The composer suggests that in performance the choirs should stand on opposite sides of the orchestra insofar as such an arrangement is practicable.

It is recommended that the men's and women's choirs be rehearsed separately and brought together only when each has become tonally secure.

He also suggests that for harmonic support four clarinets be placed among the women's choir, and similarly among the men four horns or bassoons.

The tonal textures exploited in this work are chiefly double harmonies, both diatonic and chromatic, and major triads moving in parallel chords of the tenth.

There are also three- to six-part sections in motet style for women and men.

The orchestral accompaniment, though occasionally illustrative of the text, in general supports the voices, especially in passages where the two-choir harmonies are mutually contradictive.

The Introit ("Requiem Aeternam") begins with a flowing recitative for both choirs, harmonized as parallel major chords in open positive (I, V, VII, X) and constructed melodically in such a way that the false relations of the harmony prevent any tonal or modal structure from creating intervallic tensions. As a result the line seems to flow in space. This gives us, as a locale for the liberated soul, the fullest possible amount of both space and time—in short, eternity.

These major chords of the tenth, which are also basic to organ mixture-stops, will return in the instrumental postlude.

MUSICAL ILLUSTRATIONS

MUSICAL ILLUSTRATIONS

Missa pro defunctis, Kyrie Eleison

The two choirs, each singing chords that can be heard as inversions of a dominant seventh, but also as three-note groupings from the whole-tone scale, actually produce here when singing a full-octave scale of six tones equidistant. The composer has arranged that these six tones, though heard simultaneously, are actually sung by the two choirs as separate three-note chords.

It is also to be noted that the melody, stated in a canon of chords, is the top line of these chords, the soprano and tenor voices being doubled for emphasis. The chords themselves hang from above, therefore, rather than standing on a thorough bass, or bottom line.

A bass is in general needed only for chords consistently presented in root position. Music that is more flowing, or chromatic, can benefit melodically from a top-heavy layout with respect to its harmonies.

MUSICAL ILLUSTRATIONS

MISSA PRO DEFUNCTIS

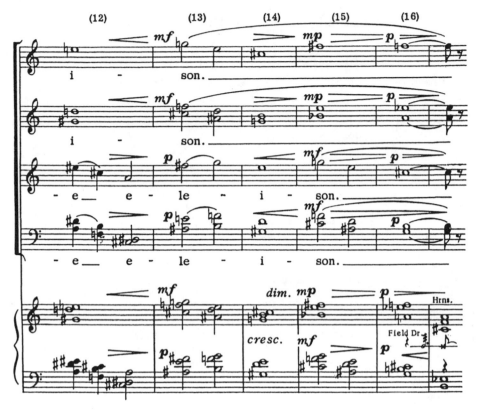

MUSICAL ILLUSTRATIONS

Missa Pro Defunctis, Sequentia (Dies Irae)

Predicting the day of Final Judgment, both choirs sing in major seconds, pianissimo misterioso, accompanied quietly by drums in a military meter.

After a short passage involving double whole-tone chords, staccato pianissimo, there are a percussive crash fortissimo and the same chords, now sung fortissimo, followed by drums only, diminuendo.

The expressive aims are mystery and terror.

MISSA PRO DEFUNCTIS

MUSICAL ILLUSTRATIONS

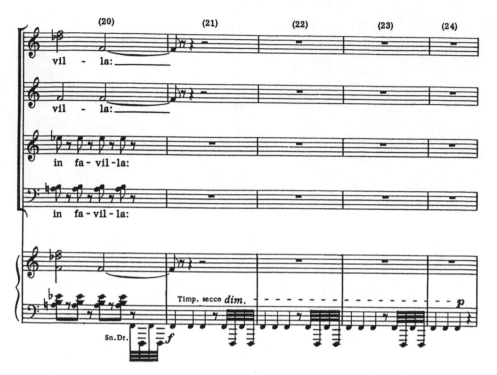

Published by H. W. Gray Co., Inc., New York.

MUSICAL ILLUSTRATIONS

Missa pro defunctis, Sanctus

Here, for male choir only, are four real parts composed in homogeneous counter-point, motet-style.

For the "Pleni sunt" passages, and the "Hosannah" which follows them, the choral treatment, though still chromatic, is more massive.

MUSICAL ILLUSTRATIONS

Published by H. W. Gray Co., Inc., New York.

MUSICAL ILLUSTRATIONS

Missa pro defunctis, Communion

This prayer for the dead is a close canon (at the octave and at a distance of only two counts) in two voices, each a major triad in close position with the top voice doubled.

The doubling here, as with chromatic chords, helps to emphasize the tune rather than the harmonies. These last merely add color to the lines, which for expressing beatitude need to float freely without the frictions or gravitational pulls that a bass-line would cause.

The canon itself, I might add, offers to the liberated soul a hint of companionship without which it might get lonesome out there forever in space.

MUSICAL ILLUSTRATIONS

MISSA PRO DEFUNCTIS

MUSICAL ILLUSTRATIONS

Missa pro defunctis, Instrumental Postlude

This brief finale in organ style uses the same thematic materials as the Prelude (not quoted).

It also imitates organ sonorities, chiefly in the use of the upper partials particular to each harmonic line, excepting the bass. This procedure involves dividing each one of the four upper string sections into four parts, each of which follows literally its leader in the brass section by playing, higher up, parallel major chords of the tenth.

This arrangement produces a sumptuosity of dissonance so resembling the organ that Manuel Rosenthal, who had conducted the work in Paris, said it sounded like Pontifical High Mass at Notre-Dame with a cardinal all in red leading the exit parade and the full organ roaring.

Which was exactly, of course, the intention.

Published by H. W. Gray Co., Inc., New York.

APPENDIX

The International Phonetic Alphabet, created in the 1880s by the International Phonetic Association, is a system for writing all the sounds currently used in spoken languages, at least in those known as Indo-European.

Each of these sounds is represented by a sign which represents that sound and no other. Combining these sounds into the strings we recognize as words or word-groups constitutes an act of performance called pronunciation. This varies with respect to both sound and meaning in French, German, and the other subgroupings we call languages. It also varies within each language, both by region and by social class.

To illustrate some of the regional variations, as these can be heard today among educated persons, I have had transcribed phonetically a familiar prose passage, the opening sentences of Abraham Lincoln's Gettysburg Address.

I am not suggesting that composers need to use this phonetic alphabet in setting verbal texts. But I do think that some acquaintance with it is likely to facilitate their work, if only in checking current standards for articulating clearly their own language.

KEY TO PHONETIC SYMBOLS

Unless otherwise indicated, all key words illustrate standard American pronunciation (Chicago).

a	back (northern England), pop	ə	sofa
ɑ	cod (New England)	ɛ	head
ɒ	hot (southern England)	f	fat
æ	cat (southern England)	g	get
ʌ	cup (southern England)	h	hen
b	bet	i	heed
d	debt	ɪ	hit
ð	thy	j	yet
e	bet	k	kin

165

APPENDIX

l l̠et

m m̠et

n n̠et

ŋ hang̲

o be̲a̲u̲ (French)

ɔ ca̲u̲ght (southern England,
    New England)

p p̠et

r r̠am

ɾ pe̲ɾ̲o (Spanish)

s s̠ue

ʃ a̲ʃ̲sure

t t̠en

θ t̠high

u o̲u̲ (French), who̲'d

ʊ ho̲o̲d

v v̠at

w w̠et

z z̠oo

ʒ A̠sia

eɪ h̠ate

ou ho̲e̲d

: [as in i:] indicates long vowel

˜ [as in ɔ̃] indicates nasalized vowel

ˌ [as in n̩] marks a consonant that
       becomes syllabic be-
       cause the vowel next
       to it is deleted in
       rapid speech

ˈ [as in ˈsevn̩] placed before syllable
       bearing main
       (word) stress

Fourscore and seven years ago our fathers brought forth on this continent a new nation conceived in liberty and dedicated to the proposition that all men are created equal. Now we are engaged in a great civil war, testing whether that nation, or any nation so conceived and so dedicated, can long endure. We are met on a great battlefield of that war.

CHICAGO

for skor ən ˈsɛvn̩ jɪrz əˈgou ɑr ˈfɑðərz brat forθ an ðɪs ˈkãn̩ent ʌ nu: ˈneiʃn̩ kənˈsi:vd ɪn ˈlɪbərɾi æn ˈdɛdɪkeiɾəd tə ðə prapəˈzɪʃn̩ ðæt ɑl mɛn ar kriˈeiɾəd ˈi:kwl̩. nau wi: ar ənˈgeidʒ̩d ɪn ʌ greit ˈsɪvl̩ wor ˈtɛstɪŋ wɛðər ðæt ˈneiʃn̩ or ɛni: ˈneiʃn̩ sou kənˈsi:vd ən sou ˈdɛdɪkeiɾəd kæn laŋ ɛnˈdur. wi: ar mɛt an ʌ greit ˈbærˌfi:ld ʌv ðæt wor.

BOSTON

fɔə skor ən ˈsɛvn̩ jɪəz əˈgou ɑuə ˈfɔðəz brat fɔθ ɔn ðɪs ˈkɔ̃n̩ent ʌ nu: ˈneiʃn̩ kənˈsi:vd ɪn ˈlɪbərɾi æn ˈdɛdɪkeiɾəd tə ðə prɔpəˈzɪʃn̩ ðæt ɔl mɛn a kriˈeiɾəd

APPENDIX

'i:kwḷ. nau wi: ar ən'geidʒd ın ʌ greit 'sıvḷ wa: 'tɛstıŋ wɛðə ðæt 'neiʃn̩ or ɛni: 'neiʃn̩ sou kən'si:vd ən sou 'dɛdıkeirəd kæn lɔŋ ɛn'djuə. wi: a mɛt ɔn ʌ greit 'bærḷfi:ld ʌv ðæt wɑ:.

DALLAS

for skor ən 'sɛvn̩ jırz ə'gɛu auə 'faðəz brɔət forθ ɔn ðıs 'kantənənt ʌ nıu 'nʌıʃn̩ kən'si:vd ın 'lıəbəti æn 'dɛdıkeirəd tə ðə prapə'zıʃn̩ ðæt ɔəl mɛən ɔr kri'eirəd 'i:kwḷ. nau wi: ɔr ən'gʌıdʒd ın ʌ grʌıt 'sıvḷ wor 'tɛstın hwɛðə ðæt 'nʌıʃn̩ or ɛni: 'nʌıʃn̩ sou kən'si:vd ən sou 'dɛdıkeirəd kæn lɔuŋ ɛn'djuə. wi: ɔr mɛət ɔn ʌ grʌıt 'bærḷfi:ld ʌv ðæt wor.

NEW ORLEANS

fɔə skɔə ən 'sɛvn̩ jıəz ə'gʌou aə 'fɔðəz brɔt fɔəθ ɔn ðıs 'kantənənt ʌ nju: 'neiʃn̩ kən'si:vd ın 'lıbəti æn 'dɛdıkeirəd tə ðə prapə'zıʃn̩ ðæt ɔl mın ɔ kri'eirəd 'i:kwḷ. nau wi: ɔr ən'geidʒd ın ʌ greit 'sıvḷ wɔ: 'tɛstın hwɛðə ðæt 'neiʃn̩ or ɛni: 'neiʃn̩ sou kən'si:vd ən sou 'dɛdıkeirəd kæn lɔŋ ɛn'djuə. wi: ɔ mɛt ɔn ʌ greit 'bærḷfi:ld ʌv ðæt wɔ:.

RICHMOND

fɔə skɔə ən 'sɛvn̩ jıəz ə'gʌu auə 'faðəz brɔət fɔəθ ɔən ðıs 'kantənənt ʌ nu: 'neiʃn̩ kən'si:vd ın 'lıbəri æn 'dɛdıkeirəd tə ðə prapə'zıʃn̩ ðæt ɔəl mın ɑ kri'eirəd 'i:kwḷ. nau wi: ar ən'geidʒd ın ʌ grʌıt 'sıvḷ wɔ: 'tɛstın hwɛðə ðæt 'neiʃn̩ or ɛni: 'neiʃn̩ sou kən'si:vd ən sou 'dɛdıkeirəd kæn lɔuŋ ɛn'djuə. wi: ɑ mɛt ɔən ʌ grʌıt 'bærḷfi:ld ʌv ðæt wɔ:.

SAN FRANCISCO

for skor ən 'sɛvn̩ jırz ə'gɛu ar 'faðərz brɔt forθ ɔn ðıs 'kõn̩ent ʌ nu: 'neiʃn̩ kən'si:vd ın 'lıbərri æn 'dɛdıkeirəd tə ðə prɔpə'zıʃn̩ ðæt ɔl mɛn ar kri'eirəd 'i:kwḷ. nau wi: ar ən'geidʒd ın ʌ greit 'sıvḷ wor 'tɛstıŋ wɛðər ðæt 'neiʃn̩ or

APPENDIX

ɛni: 'neiʃn̩ sou kən'si:vd ən sou 'dɛdɪkeirəd kæn laŋ ɛn'dur. wi: ar mɛt ɔn ʌ greit 'bær|fi:ld ʌv ðæt wor.

RECEIVED PRONUNCIATION (England)

'fɔ: skɔ:r ən 'sɛvn̩ 'jɪəz ə'gəu ɑ: 'fɑ:ðəz 'brɔ:t 'fɔ:θ ɒn ðɪs 'kɒntɪnənt ə 'nju: 'neɪʃn̩ kən'si:vd ɪn 'lɪbətɪ ən 'dɛdɪkeɪtɪd tə ðə 'prɒpə'zɪʃn̩ ðət 'ɔ:l men ə krɪ'eɪtɪd 'i:kwəl. 'nau wɪ ər ɪn'geɪdʒd ɪn ə 'greɪt 'sɪv| 'wɔ: 'testɪŋ wɛðə 'ðæt 'neɪʃn̩ ɔ:r 'ɛnɪ 'neɪʃn̩ 'səu kən'si:vd ən 'səu 'dɛdɪkeɪtɪd kən 'lɒŋ ɪn'djuə. wi: ə 'mɛt ɒn ə 'greɪt 'bæt|fi:ld əv ðæt 'wɔ:.

SCOTLAND

'fo:r sko:r ən 'sɛvn̩ 'ji:rz ə'go: ʌur 'faðərz 'brɔt 'forθ ɒn ðɪs 'kɒntɪnənt ə 'nju: 'neʃn̩ kən'si:vd ɪn 'lɪbərte ən 'dɛdɪketəd tə ðə 'prɔpə'zɪʃn̩ ðət 'ɔl mɛn ər kri'etəd 'ikwəl. 'nʌu wi ər ən'gedʒd ɪn ə 'gret 'sɪv| 'wɔ:r 'tɛstɪŋ hwɛðər 'ðat 'neʃn̩ ɔr 'ɛne 'neʃn̩ 'so: kən'si:vd ən 'so: 'dɛdɪketəd kən 'lɔŋ ən'dʒu:r. wi ər 'mɛt ɔn ə 'gret 'bat|fild əv ðat 'wɔ:r.

A SHORT READING-LIST

As was remarked earlier, this is not a textbook; it is a how-to book by a workman with experience in both writing and performing vocal music. Its aim is to share some of that experience with other workmen, viewing the subject from a composer's point of view. Any composer's extra time, I think, is best spent with music itself, both classical and modern, and with reading what other composers have written about their working methods.

There is not as much of this last as one might wish; but it is precious, all of it, as it turns up in Mozart's letters, for instance, and in Richard Wagner's autobiography *Mein Leben* (Munich, 1911; trans. in E. Newman, *Fact and Fiction about Wagner* [London, 1931]). In the memoirs of Hector Berlioz (Paris, 1870; ed. and trans. D. Cairns, London, 1969) there is less of it than of attention to his literary sources. But the published correspondence between Strauss and his librettist, *Richard Strauss und Hugo von Hofmannsthal: Briefwechsel: Gesamtausgabe* (Zurich, 1952; trans. Hanns Hammelmann and Ewald Osers as *A Working Friendship: The Correspondence between Richard Strauss and Hugo von Hoffmannsthal* [New York, 1961]) is full of revelations. So is Wilfrid Mellers's *Harmonious Meeting: A Study of the Relationship between English Music, Poetry and Theatre, ca. 1600–1900* (London, 1960).

On the purely musical side, but still by composers, I suggest the treatise on composing with twelve tones *Introduction à la musique de douze sons* by René Leibowitz (Paris, 1949). Also the *Thesaurus of Scales and Melodic Patterns* by Nicolas Slonimsky (New York, 1947); and *Technique de mon langage musical* by Olivier Messiaen (Paris, 1944; trans. John Satterfield, 1957).

The most useful orchestration books are practically all by composers, from the *Grand traité d'instrumentation et d'orchestration modernes* of Berlioz (Paris, 1844) and its modernization by Richard Strauss in *Treatise on Instrumentation* (published together in a trans. by Theodore Front, New York, 1948); to *Principes d'orchestration* (Paris, 1921), a two-volume work by Nikolay Rimsky-Korsakov illustrated by his own music; to the handbook *Technique de l'orchestre moderne* by Charles-Marie Widor (Paris, 1904), indispensible for its listing of all the intervals and chords that are practical for stringed instruments. The general compendia *Orchestration* by Cecil Forsyth (London, 1914), *Orchestration* by Walter Piston (New York, 1955), and *Thesaurus of Orchestral Devices* by Gardner Read (New York, 1953) are also handy to have around.

Certain works of sheer scholarship, but written from the composers' point of view, are also valuable. Among these I recommend *J. S. Bach* by Albert Schweitzer (trans. from the German by Ernest Newman, New York, 1958) and *Rhythmic Gesture in Mozart: "Le Nozze di Figaro" and "Don Giovanni"* by Wye Jamison Allanbrook (Chicago, 1983). *Rhythm and Tempo: A Study in Music History* by Curt Sachs (New York, 1953) is also very much worth reading, and so are *Le lied romantique allemand* (Paris, 1956) and *Wagner et le wagnérisme* (Paris, 1946), both by Marcel Beaufils.

Additional titles are *The Pronunciation of English* by Daniel Jones (Cambridge, England, 1958); *The Singing Voice* by Robert Rushmore (New York, 1984); *The Singer's Manual of English Diction* by Madeleine Marshall (New York, 1946); and *French Grand Opera: An Art and a Business* by William L.Crosten (New York, 1948), which exposes the power structure clear down to the *chef de claque* at the Paris Opera, which seems to have become by 1830 the first of the great modern houses.

Composing in Latin for the Catholic liturgy is scarcely worth the trouble nowadays, since the ecumencial council known as Vatican II abolished its use in 1963. This turn toward services in the vernacular has proved generally acceptable almost everywhere but in France, where the language itself resists being chanted, and is not musically comfortable in liturgical set-pieces either.

A similar abolition of Latin in the Anglican liturgy had taken place much earlier, under Henry VIII. When this monarch broke with Rome, he took over Church properties, thus making it possible to go on holding services, albeit in English, and to keep the great choirs functioning.

A huge job was here set out for translators, as well as for composers; but they seem to have taken it up with energy and dispatch. The prayer book of the 1650s named for Edward VI provided a handsome English text. A new translation of the whole Bible was also begun at about this time. And a method for singing in English the psalms and canticles—the ever-so-ingenious Anglican chant—had been created, and the composition of motets and anthems got well under way within less than half a century. Services in the vernacular were in England a popular success, though most of

Ireland had stayed Catholic; and Scotland, stubborn as usual, turned Calvinist. The composers of England even found time (and a busy market) for madrigals and glees, theatrical songs, and all sorts of music for masques.

The English masters from the sixteenth century till the death of Purcell at the end of the seventeenth, in 1695, produced vocal music of remarkable variety and flavor. And within another fifty years, George Frideric Handel, a German composer trained in Italy, had pulled it all together, including the setting of English, into a style of vocal composition, still using the big choirs, that has survived to this day. Styles in instrumental accompaniment have changed constantly, as they always do. But the English vocal line in Benjamin Britten's twentieth-century operas, and, for all its debt to American rock-pop, that of the Beatles, would still, I am sure, be found acceptable by Handel himself.

Vocal music in America has followed for the most part a different model. Our early psalm books, our "white spirituals" and fuguing-tunes, gospel ditties, blues, torch-songs, and show-tunes (the mating-music of our musical comedies, which tends ever to follow the rhythmic patterns of social dancing)—all this is different here, except for the mating-music. And for sedate hymns, which follow a British model perfected in the eighteenth century, with Handelian harmonies and Handelian verbal prosody.

Opera composition in the United States has tended toward historical subjects like Salem witchcraft, as in Robert Ward's *Crucible,* and Douglas Moore's regionally picturesque *Ballad of Baby Doe* (about early Colorado) and *Carrie Nation* (which deals with the temperance movement in Kansas). Marc Blitzstein's *Cradle Will Rock* and his cantata *No for an Answer* are political tracts. Such, too, is my own (with Gertrude Stein) *Mother of Us All,* while George Gershwin's *Porgy and Bess* and my *Four Saints in Three Acts* (the latter also with Gertrude Stein) are saturated with homage to the Negro voice.

As regards texts written *for* music, I strongly recommend *Words for Music* by V. C. Clinton-Baddeley (Cambridge, England, 1941) and *The Tenth Muse* by Patrick J. Smith (New York, 1970), a history of opera librettos.

All these books and many others can make good reading, but I still insist that composers avoid overindulgence in mere information, and that they save their eyes (and ears) for music itself.

INDEX

Accentuation. *See* Stresses

Accompaniment, instrumental, 13, 30, 37–43, 74–75, 76; to duets, 23; to recitative, 22

Acting, by singers, 68

Albee, Edward, 58

Alberti bass, 75

Allanbrook, Wye Jamison, 170

American English, 3, 4, 13, 51

Anglican church, 27, 170

Anthem, 23

Aria, 22–23, 24, 74

Arioso, 22

Arpeggio, 44, 75

Auden, W. H., 70, 72

Australian speech, 60

Bach, Johann Sebastian, 34–35, 38, 54, 57

Ballad of Baby Doe, The (Moore), 61, 171

Ballet, 23

Ballo in maschera, Un (Verdi), 68*n*

Barber, Samuel, 60

Barber of Seville, The (Rossini), 54, 67

Barraud, Henry, 61

Bate, Stanley, 62

Beatles, 171

Beaufils, Marcel, 170

Beethoven, Ludwig van, 57; concert songs by, 24; *Fidelio,* 38, 39–41, 55; Symphony no. *3,* 45; Symphony no. *5,* 46

"Before Sleeping" (Thomson), 89–91

Bel canto, 67

Bellini, Vincenzo, 68

Berg, Alban, 58

Berlioz, Hector, 68, 169

Berners, Lord, 62

Billy the Kid (Copland), 65

Birthday Bouquet, A (Stein), 58

Bizet, Georges, 32*n*, 62

Blake, William, 17, 18, 19, 21, 33

Blitzstein, Marc, 55, 60, 171

Blues, 30

Boris Godunov (Mussorgsky), 65

Brahms, Johannes, 4–5, 24, 48

Brazilian Portuguese, 24, 27

Britten, Benjamin, 55, 58, 60, 62, 171

Byron, Lord, 57

Caccini, Giulio, 51*n*

Cadence, of language, 4, 9, 12, 26

Cage, John, 102

Calder, Alexander, 38

Canadian speech, 60

Cantata, 64

Canterbury Tales (Chaucer), 33

Carmen (Bizet), 32*n*, 62

Carrie Nation (Moore), 171

Caruso, Enrico, 36

Catholic liturgy, 50

Cenerentola, La (Rossini), 65

Chaliapin, Feodor, 36

Chamber music, x, 25

Chaucer, Geoffrey, 33

Chekhov, Anton, 58

Chest voice, 31

Chinese language, 4

Chopin, Frédéric, 30

Choral music, ix, 23–24, 25, 46

Church chanting, 8, 22, 27

Claudel, Paul, 70

Clinton-Baddeley, V. C., 171

Coleridge, Samuel Taylor, 57

Coloratura, 7, 68*n*

Comic opera, 64

Communist Manifesto, 24

Concerted pieces, 23

Concert song, ix, 24, 31

Consonants, 9–10, 11–12, 29

Consul, The (Menotti), 55

Countermelody, 37

173

INDEX

INDEX